VICTORIA HENRICH

PRACTICE *makes* POSITIVE

PRIORITIZE HAPPINESS TEN MINUTES AT A TIME

SHINE
PRESS

Published by: Shine Press
4522 W Village Dr. Unit #1294 Tampa, FL 33624

For permission requests and sharing information, contact:
Shine-Press.com

Book Cover Designer: Michelle Sucher

Paperback ISBN: 979-8-9909367-6-8

F I R S T   E D I T I O N

Shine Press offers writing, editing, designing, publishing,
and marketing services, focusing on high quality at
affordable prices with an excellent author experience.

Contact us for more information about our personalized Spark Books,
publishing packages, book marketing, and Bestseller Campaign.

*To those on the path to happiness —
may you discover that the journey
is as beautiful as the destination.*

Contents

Prologue

HELLO FELLOW HUMAN!

I completely appreciate you being here. I hope you enjoy this journal of my thoughts and insights into how I find happiness while living within my vibration.

My entire life, people have told me that I smile all the time, that I'm happy, and that things always seem to work out for me. They say they wish they could bottle up some of my energy and drink it. Okay, that last one might be a little weird, but I'm sure it's meant well.

In a world filled with societal divisions, negativity, social media pressure, rising mental health crisis, and increased isolation caused by technology, happiness can be hard to find. With today's cancel culture, fear often dominates our thoughts and decisions. We're so worried about doing the wrong thing that we don't know how to do what's right for us.

Happiness isn't something you just stumble upon anymore—it requires seeking, recognizing, and embracing it when you find it. This book is about making small adjustments in perception to train your brain to see things in a happier light. It's about using a positive lens to find joy in everyday moments.

Honestly, I used to think that was how everyone lived. But as I've grown older and listened to more stories from the world, I've realized that not everyone sees things this way. I may be a little different—and you are too. We're all different. So, this is my attempt to share how I process life's experiences and turn them into happiness. My "secret sauce" for happiness is detailed in these pages, so stick with me.

Like many of you, I've faced life events that have tested my happiness. Having children has brought me immense joy, but raising them hasn't always been easy. Worrying about them and the world they've grown up in can make sleep hard to come by. Kids will make you question every decision you make.

I've also gone through a divorce. I've moved, been unemployed, and changed jobs. I've been a stay-at-home mom, which I found to be one of the hardest—and loneliest—things I've ever done. I've lost my parents.

So, how is it possible to maintain happiness and a positive outlook when life is filled with challenges and disappointments? Well, I'll tell you how I do it!

People often ask me if I'm always this happy, why I'm so happy, and if I'd share whatever I'm drinking so they could feel this happy too. Well, this book is the roadmap to how my brain works—my secret to happiness. Some of you may not connect with it, and that's okay. Try another book that speaks to you. But maybe, just maybe, one little thing in here will resonate. That one small spark might lead you to everything already within you. Everything you need might be ready to come out, and perhaps all you needed was a gentle acknowledgment or validation.

This book is about who I am, my internal thoughts, and how I choose to live my life by embracing my vibration and practicing positivity. But more importantly, it's a book for you—to help you discover what makes you happy, how to leverage your vibration, and how practice can bring positivity into your life too.

It's an easy read—nothing scientific—simple enough for you to take what you like and apply it to your life immediately. Maybe try it on for a while and see how it feels.

We all have a true purpose and a unique vibration that comes from deep inside. We are happiest when we live in that true vibration, fulfill our purpose, and do what we love with the people we love. When we're connected to the world, part of a community, and in tune with ourselves, we find happiness. Easy, right?

I hope this book helps you reconnect with your vibration. Living within your vibration doesn't necessarily mean wealth—though that may be a nice side effect. But living your true vibration will make you happy.

I truly hope you get to where you want to be. For me, everything is about happiness. Everything. I prioritize happiness. I love happiness. I don't want to be anything other than happy.

SHOULDN'T WE ALL WANT TO BE HAPPY?

Discovering Vibration

"Victoria, get in here right now!" This wasn't the first time my mom had yelled at me, but the intense panic in her voice frightened me as a ten-year-old.

"Victoria, you stay in your room!" My dad's voice was tense in a way I'd never heard before. He was dropping me off after a weekend visit with him. They were in the throes of a bitter divorce.

My parents were talking in the kitchen, and I was putting my things away in my room when the shouting started. I slowly walked out of my room and looked toward the kitchen, but I couldn't see anyone. I heard them mumbling. Unsure of what I would find, I bravely made my way around the corner to see my dad straddling my mom on the floor with a knife to her throat. This was one of their bad moments when their emotions took over. They were feeling out of control and threatened by the one person they trusted the most; each other.

My parents loved me. They loved each other. We had a nice home in a quiet neighborhood. I took dance classes and had pets. We enjoyed laughter together and I felt very loved by them. Sure, it wasn't perfect. Maybe they drank a little too much. Maybe they fought a little too much. Maybe they used me as a pawn in their games against each other a little too much. But I'd never been involved in their arguments.

They decided I would be the best person to determine what should happen next. My mother wanted me to call the police, but my father informed me that if I did, he would probably go to jail, and I would never see him again. So, what did I do? I decided I was unable to decide.

I screamed at the top of my lungs and fell to the floor. And it worked. They both ran over to me apologizing and I kept screaming for quite a while. I didn't want to hear what they had to say anymore, so I drowned them out with my voice. Honestly, I think I freaked them out a little bit. I did not want to be brought into this fight, and I chose not to participate.

A few months later my mother had slipped into a deep depression. She ultimately wanted to reconnect with my father, but he was unwilling. There was too much damage between them. One evening I woke up in the back of her car. My mother had placed me there while I was sleeping. The shutting of the back seat door and her getting into the driver's seat woke me up. I somehow instinctively knew what her next steps would be. She was crying. The car was in the garage and the garage door was shut. The lights were off, but I could see her hand on the ignition. She was contemplating turning the car on. I gently touched her shoulder and whispered to her that I wasn't ready to die and that I didn't think she was either.

I often wonder how I knew so much at the age of ten. I'm thinking it was all the TV dramas and soap operas I watched with my mother and grandmother. There was always someone cheating, plotting a murder, or contemplating suicide in almost every episode. Maybe that's why I was able to lead her out of that car that night.

TAKING NOTES

These two pivotal moments in my childhood taught me to separate the things that were happening around me from the things that were happening to me. I somehow figured out that my life was separate from theirs and that I needed to focus on my future and the steps I would take to get there.

PRACTICE *makes* POSITIVE

We all have some form of childhood trauma, although I truly despise those words. As children, we tend to remember the bad. All parents have difficult days and heated exchanges, and most kids witness at least one firsthand. Those experiences can be frightening and life-altering because, to a child, parents are the leaders—the ones who are supposed to have the answers. It's unsettling to see them lose control. Yet, in the grand timeline of our lives, these instances are often brief. Hopefully, for most of us, our parents get it right more often than they get it wrong.

At the tender age of ten, I began taking notes on what I wanted and what I didn't want for my future. I began finding an internal vibration that was distinctly mine. It wasn't my mother's or my father's, it was mine. I could control, protect, and fuel it. My vibration became my safe space. When I focused on it, I couldn't hear the toxic noise around me.

So far in the life of Victoria, with these two childhood experiences, I learned to focus and count on my own vibration, and to be selective of what I let into my heart and mind. I discovered how to control and process my emotions more.

In the next section, we'll explore vibration together so you can reveal yours—without all the family drama. And I promise, the rest of my stories are more upbeat and fun.

WHAT THE HECK IS VIBRATION, ANYWAY?

What is your vibration and how do you find it? Your vibration is your gift. It's what comes naturally for you. It's who you are at the core level. It's what makes you uniquely you. You discover it by being yourself and getting to know the real you.

The obstacle is when our vibration gets muted by outside forces. It's always there, but it doesn't overpower the other noises around us. Obligations and other's louder presence can distract us. Our sense of self is drowned out. Make time to reconnect with your vibe— listen to it and nurture it. It is you.

Being a child, I could have chosen to let my parents' struggles become my own. I could have absorbed their vibration of drama instead of putting up a force field, protecting my own.

This book is full of personal stories and suggestions to help you connect with your vibration and take full advantage of its power.

You might ask, "What makes you knowledgeable about living your vibration?" My answer: life lessons and an eighth-grade Psychology class. The teacher introduced us to the ILAC sign, an acronym for 'I am lovable and capable.' She explained that every human has an ILAC sign, which can be strengthened or weakened through interaction. Our words and actions affect others' ILAC signs, just as they shape our own.

Most importantly, our internal dialogue plays a key role in building or tearing down our ILAC sign. The biggest takeaway I hope you get from this book? Be kind to yourself. Nurture your ILAC sign. It's your little light!

That teacher had us practice building up each other's ILAC signs, as well as our own, and then reflect on how it felt. For me, it felt amazing—like I was unlocking a secret superpower. I loved knowing that a small action, a kind word, or a simple gesture could shift someone's day. Maybe it did, maybe it didn't, but believing it did made all the difference. I pictured myself scattering little sparks of sunshine wherever I went, trusting that someone, somewhere, was picking them up.

That's when it clicked—this was my purpose. This was the moment everything started for me. I became hyper-aware of ILAC and the quiet influence I carried as one small person in a big world. I started noticing invisible love tanks—mine, theirs, everyone's—and just how easy it was to fill them. A smile, a compliment, a tiny act of kindness—it all mattered. And from that point on, I made it my mission to lift ILAC signs higher, to spread that energy everywhere I could.

I've been practicing ever since.

I became a kind of feelings connoisseur. Dare I say, it's become a personal mission of mine to help others feel better before they even recognize their own feelings. Sometimes, I'm spot on, and other times, I completely miss the mark. Some people make it clear they're closed off to my energy—and that's okay too. I simply sprinkle goodness where I can and move along. I do it because it makes me happy. It makes my vibration hum! And that is a truly wonderful feeling.

This is the light others see in me, the one they sometimes question. Is she really this happy? Is she faking it? Why is she so happy all the time? For me, I'm a happiness fairy. The best part of this wild, joyful energy I carry is that I don't need anyone else to create this vortex of love—it's entirely my own. I put it out there, and am content in doing so. That's why I constantly smile—I'm dropping little balls of sunshine your way.

Over time, I came to understand that it wasn't just a sign, a destination, or even a tank to fill or draw from. It's more of a flow—a connection between thoughts, actions, words, and feelings. I labeled it vibration. To me, it's the energy to exude, the vibe to put out into the world. It's the first thing people pick up on when they're around—the unique rhythm that moves in and out, bouncing off and blending with others' rhythms. In that exchange, we feel good, bad, or indifferent.

Call it whatever feels right to you, but know this—it's the best version of who you are. It's how you interact with the world when you strip away the noise of judgment and obligation.

It should be the most important thing in the world to you. Your vibration is your true self, yet most people don't even know how to find it or listen to it. You might wonder: Who am I? What do I have to offer the world? What is my calling or purpose? But remember, your purpose doesn't have to be Nobel Peace Prize-worthy. Mine is spreading imaginary sunshine to whoever needs it. It's simply whatever connects you to your happiness.

FOUR THINGS I KNOW ABOUT MY VIBRATION

I am a person who has reinvented myself a few times. I am a business owner. I am a dreamer. I am a wife. I am a friend. I am a mother. And I was a daughter. Also—I'm a new grandmother!

I've always been a rule follower. From as early as I can remember, I trusted the people around me to know more than I did, so I assumed they knew what was best. I never really questioned what I was told. I also learned that if I tried my best and behaved as expected—by family, culture, and society—I would be respected and even admired. This worked in childhood, but as I experienced more of life, I started to drift from those expectations.

The first thing I knew about my vibration was that it fueled my ability to work hard and stand on my own. So, at around 20, I shocked my entire family by leaving Florida and moving to Virginia. The little rule follower went rogue. I was ready to fly.

The second thing I knew I could trust about my vibration was the fearlessness it gave me. I wasn't afraid of change. I wasn't afraid of taking a chance. I wasn't afraid of starting over or proving myself and my abilities. I had big plans. I was heading toward a doctorate in Industrial Psychology. I wanted to travel the country, working for a big corporate company, conducting training programs, and focusing on employee morale. This was the early '90s—long before it became trendy. I was going to be Corporate Barbie.

(Side note: I spent years of my childhood playing make-believe with Barbie, working through endless life scenarios with her. Maybe I was just in training all along!)

Then something wonderfully unexpected happened. Just as I was applying for graduate school, I became pregnant with my first child. And everything changed. My entire world became her. Even the pregnancy itself consumed me—I was completely absorbed in becoming her mom. My vibration beat only for her. Suddenly, the world was different. Food tasted different. Smells were different. My focus had shifted entirely.

PRACTICE *makes* POSITIVE

I wanted to give her the best life I could. All I wanted to be was Mommy Barbie—and that's exactly what I became. It was amazing. My vibration never felt stronger than when I was parenting my five children. It will always be my most cherished adventure.

The third truth I knew about my vibration was that it helped me see life as an adventure. I never felt the need to conform to societal norms. My focus in life was simple: be happy. Find what makes me happy and do more of it—while avoiding what doesn't. That is the foundation of who I am. My core vibration.

Luckily, I'm easily made happy. Simple things bring me joy. Making others happy makes me happy. Cliché? I know.

The fourth thing I knew about my vibration was that it reinforced my belief that what's meant to be will be. I believe there's more good in the world than bad, and that if I just do the right thing, good things will happen. It makes life pretty simple and uncomplicated. I love life. I love experiencing love and friendship. I just love love itself, and I trust in the goodness of people and the world. I know that can be a bit naive, but so far, it's worked out just fine for me.

Also—I tend to forget the bad stuff. I just seem to erase it from my mind. So, if you think I'm mad at you, I'm not. I've literally forgotten what happened. Let's be friends.

Ultimately, I am a dreamer, and I am a survivor. I will always find a way to get where I want to be, do what I want to do, and spend time with the people I love. There is no greater purpose for me. I don't take no for an answer—I just find another way.

I prioritize what makes me happy while trying every day to stay kind and humble. I search for who I am, striving to see, hear, and feel my vibration so I can live to my fullest potential—the purpose I was born to fulfill. At the end of the day, all I have to give is me.

I know I drive some people crazy—I can't help it! It's who I am. But here's the thing: we can only be who we are. We're not meant to be like anyone else. That's the journey—finding our path, our calling. For me, it's about being the best version of myself and fully embracing this life before it's over.

Now that you know a little more about me—my background, my vibration—let's dig a little deeper into life things.

Change is Going to Happen

Change bothers us. It unsettles us. Often, we get so comfortable in our normalcy that we accept being unhappy or unfulfilled—simply because the fear of the unknown feels more uncomfortable than staying the same. We choose mediocrity over change.

But here's the thing—everything evolves, and so do we. You cannot live the same day over and over again. It's never the same day!

Maybe you wake up and your child is sick. Maybe there's a pileup on the interstate, and you have to take a different route. Maybe you're on vacation, and you start your morning with a mimosa instead of your laptop! Every day is different, even in the smallest ways.

The people you interact with are also having different days—so your interactions will shift, too. You might have a terrible encounter with someone one day, only to have a remarkable one with them the next. If your spouse is working late on a deadline, if your child is auditioning for a school play, if your boss is knee-deep in annual reviews—you adjust.

That's life. Change is constant, and we are wired to adapt. We all have a vibration that connects and interacts with the world around us. The more we embrace the shifts, the smoother our rhythm becomes.

One day, years ago, I woke up focused on all the things I thought were important that day. It was my daughter's birthday, and I was bringing cupcakes to her preschool. I also needed to take my mother to a doctor's appointment before heading off to a full day of work, packed with appointments and deadlines. My mind was consumed with logistics—I was on autopilot, juggling my responsibilities and trying to fit everything and everyone into my schedule. I remember feeling stretched and stressed. We've all been there. Busy, busy, busy.

And then—everything changed.

My mom started speaking in jumbled words. They were the right words, just in the wrong order. Her inflection was normal, her facial expressions were normal—but her words didn't make sense. In that moment, I knew she was having a stroke.

Nothing else mattered.

Suddenly, everything that had consumed my thoughts just minutes before became completely insignificant. I adjusted in an instant.

Not all adjustments in life will be this clearly defined. Sometimes, you won't know the best way to pivot in the moment. Life emergencies will happen, but the more in tune you are with yourself and your vibration, the better you'll be at navigating change. Instead of living on autopilot, you'll start to feel more in control.

We've all had that feeling—that nagging sense that something is off, but we can't quite put our finger on it. This usually happens when something within us has shifted—when what we once loved no longer brings us joy, when something we used to connect with suddenly feels out of rhythm. And in those moments, we start to question ourselves: What's wrong with me?

As humans, we tend to crave routine, but sometimes we need a little excitement to shake things up. Prioritizing other people's flow over your own can leave you feeling empty and drained. This could be a boss, your children, a significant other—even your pets can get bossy! If you don't make your happiness a priority, at least sometimes, you risk creating a void that can grow dangerously large. Ignoring your natural desires and happiness for too long pulls you further from your true self.

You are meant to dance to your own vibration. It's what gives life meaning, what brings you joy, what feels good and right. Your vibration has a natural rhythm that needs to stay in tune for your well-being. We all have a purpose and a path to our heart's desire, and staying in alignment with that path requires constant movement and adjustment. You should always be flowing with your vibration, striving to be the best and happiest version of yourself.

For example:

- If you don't like how an interaction with a loved one went yesterday, adjust how you approach it today to make tomorrow better.

- If you don't like the way your pants fit, make a small change in what you eat today to feel better tomorrow.

- If you're unhappy with your current situation, take steps today—however small—to move closer to the happiness you desire.

Like little orphan Annie always said, "Tomorrow, tomorrow, I love ya, tomorrow, you're always a day away." Cheesy, but true. You can't change the past. You can only change tomorrow. But it takes action today to create the tomorrow you want. If you don't make changes, you'll remain exactly where you are. The sooner you give yourself room to adjust, the sooner you'll return to happiness and your true vibration. And remember—this is a journey, not a destination.

Feeling lost, frustrated, irritated, overwhelmed, or disconnected from your work or life isn't a sign of failure. It's simply a sign that you've evolved and may need to move on from what no longer serves you. The energy you bring to your present will shape your future.

But don't feel overwhelmed by the idea of change. Take your time. Get to know yourself and your vibration. And most importantly—keep in mind that this takes practice.

TIMING IS EVERYTHING

Sometimes, you may need to take a break from something, while other times, a little tweaking is all that's needed. I know I'm on the wrong path—or pushing for something that isn't meant for me—when everything just feels hard. No matter what I do, I can't seem to get anywhere. It's like swimming upstream, struggling against the current, unable to catch a break. That's when I know: this isn't my time or space.

Sometimes, the signs are small but clear. Take shopping, for example. If I try to leave the house and, just as I step outside, my dog bolts down the street, forcing me into a wild chase—fine, no big deal. But then I finally get in the car, spill water all over myself, and have to go back inside to change. Just as I'm about to head out again, a family member calls with a problem. At that point, it's obvious: today is not my shopping day. When I finally surrender to the timing, I usually end up happier in the end.

That doesn't mean it's all or nothing. Sometimes, you just need a different approach or a little patience. Maybe I will go shopping another day, or I switch to online shopping instead! The key is to listen to the energy around you and move in harmony with the natural flow of things.

Timing can have everything to do with it. I've wanted to write a book my entire life—it's just always been in the back of my mind. At one point, I even wrote the first chapter of an action-adventure novel. I still plan to finish that one someday. Fiction is harder than you'd think!

My first book idea came about 25ish years ago. I thought I was pretty good at potty training. I had all my children trained by the age of two, mainly because I started introducing them to the concept early. Most people begin at age two, but by then, you've missed that sweet spot for learning. The problem was, I could write a pretty good pamphlet or short how-to manual, but not an entire book. It wasn't my time.

In my twenties, I wanted to teach elementary education and work my way up to principal someday, but it was just not in the cards at the time. I wanted it badly enough that I earned my master's degree while home with two children under five. But the timing was not right.

I wanted true friendships at an early age, certain romantic relationships to work out, and the life I dreamed of in second grade. In some ways, I was achieving what I wanted, but in other instances, it just wasn't the right time. I had to wait. It's not always what you want that's the problem, it's the timing—and wanting it right now—that might be the issue. It helps to practice awareness and patience.

In our twenties, we want it all—our dreams, our milestones, right then and there. But sometimes, we must wait. That doesn't mean giving up on those dreams. Continue to plan for them. Envision them, nurture them, and hold them close. The world will deliver them to you at the right time, but you need to stay open. Make micro-movements to stay on course.

I have a friend who struggled with infertility for decades. She recently had a baby through surrogacy in her late forties. You might take the long road to get there, but if you keep your dreams in mind, you will get there eventually. It might not look exactly like you imagined, but you can get there. Just don't get stuck where you don't want to be. Don't let everyday obligations overpower you so much that you forget yourself completely. Keep nurturing your dreams and make baby steps toward them over time. Keep your dreams in perspective, and when you can't see a path to them anymore, change.

My daughter wanted to be in the medical field since she was a little girl. She loved helping her grandmother with different ailments and going with her to doctor's appointments. She would watch Grey's Anatomy and other medical shows over and over again. During her senior photo session, she even dressed in scrubs and wore a stethoscope.

When my nephew was in college, also wanting to enter the medical profession, he would stay with us for a night or two and teach her and my son medical terms and tell them interesting stories. I know these visits made a lasting impression. He was in college, and they were in their early high school years. His visits were magical. He would even teach them to ballroom dance right in our kitchen! Extended family can be so important.

My nephew is now a doctor, and my daughter is in her last semester of nursing school. Her ultimate goal is to become a nurse anesthetist. It's a long road with many milestones to achieve, but she is slowly getting there. I admire her steadfast perseverance. She's faced many obstacles, including a global pandemic, but she constantly adjusts to stay on the path. Things might slow her down, and she seems to find the more challenging routes, but she does what she needs to do to keep taking steps toward her goal.

We have a saying in our home: "Shoot for the moon and fall amongst the stars." I'm sure you've heard it too. For us, it means to dream as big as you can imagine and end up somewhere pretty amazing along the way. But who knows, you might even make it all the way. She's one to persevere through the Milky Way!

Colonel Sanders, the man who created Kentucky Fried Chicken, didn't become a professional chef until he was 40, after decades of failed businesses. He didn't franchise until he was 62 and didn't become an icon until after he sold his company at 75. Vera Wang started her fashion line at 40 after being passed over for a promotion to editor-in-chief.

Once you make simple shifts, you can look at each situation from a new perspective. Have you ever watched the movie Sliding Doors? The main character gets fired from her job and takes the train home. In one parallel, she makes the train and arrives home to find her boyfriend in bed with another woman. She faces two horrible tragedies: getting fired and discovering her boyfriend's infidelity. However, she ends up meeting a wonderful man, landing a fantastic job, and her life improves. In the other parallel, she misses the train and gets home after the mistress has left. Although the couple stays together, the main character constantly questions his fidelity and takes several low-paying jobs. Her life becomes miserable, and the affair continues. Sometimes, the tragedy we face becomes the catapult that takes us to true happiness. When you're craving change, sometimes you can achieve it with little effort. Small movements can keep you on course or take you in a completely new direction, so be mindful every day.

Don't be afraid to shake things up. At work, it can be as easy as parking in a different spot and taking a longer walk to the building, decluttering your desk, or asking to be part of a new project. At home, it could be rearranging your furniture, switching up household chores or carpool duties, or even changing the day you do laundry. It may seem simple, but it keeps your brain awake.

We shift as space and time shift. Sometimes, we drift too far off our resting vibration and things just feel off. Your resting vibration is simply who you are in your most quiet, natural moments. It's when you're comfortable and not trying to impress anyone or achieve anything. It's easy. It's the true you. Try to notice this resting vibration and return to it as often as possible. Your resting vibration is your true center. When something feels out of alignment, shake things up slightly and see if your perspective changes.

We are creatures of habit. We tend to park in the same area, sit at the same lunch table, and order the same favorites. We interact with the same people, eat the same foods, and even use the same burner on our stovetop. However, this doesn't change our perspective. We see and do the same things over and over, and life just becomes boring. It sounds crazy, but the smallest changes can make huge ripples in the world, which can change everything. You might meet someone new, see a new opportunity, or find a new favorite thing.

You can take a different class at the gym or try going at a different time or day for a few days. Instead of going through the drive-thru at your favorite coffee shop, park and go inside. Maybe take the stairs instead of the elevator for a month. At the carpool line, park and walk up instead of staying in your car. With these simple changes, you'll meet a whole new set of people, have completely different experiences, and shift your vibration. You might even meet your new best friend, your soul mate, or stumble upon your future business venture. Stay open and move around within your space. Break free from the repetition, even in the slightest way. That alone can make you a happier person.

ACCEPTABLE CHANGE

We deal with change every day, yet so many of us are afraid of it, whether we realize it or not. Some people call themselves "change-averse," but I call them out. Why? Because we deal with change every darn day. Some change is easy or acceptable, while other change goes against everything we want. You might be surprised by the acceptable changes you already navigate each day without hesitation.

Take the weather, for example. It changes all the time. Every day can be drastically different. Some days, it creates an inconvenience—you might need to cancel plans or grab an umbrella. Some days it makes you sad, others it makes you happy, but you accept that each day will be different. You even expect it to be.

You probably have an app that tells you what to expect from the weather each day, but you're not nervous or overwhelmed by these changes, are you? Probably not. You simply make minor adjustments accordingly and accept what happens. Maybe you grab a raincoat, wear shoes you don't mind getting wet, or skip the car wash. You hardly give it much thought. It's just a minor adjustment to accommodate the shift.

Of course, natural disasters are a totally different story. We live in Florida, so occasionally we have hurricanes that we need to prepare for. Luckily, we're far enough inland that we don't need to worry about storm surges, but we do need to prepare for power outages, water contamination, high winds, and tornadoes. We pull in our patio furniture and make sure we have plenty of supplies. Businesses close to give people the opportunity to prepare, and schools close to become hurricane shelters for those in need.

Although we understand the severity and potential damage these storms can cause, for the most part, we're used to it. As crazy as it sounds, we actually enjoy parts of it. It brings a break from the everyday routine. Everyone's off work, the weather is usually nice before the storm comes, and neighbors are outside helping each other board up windows or tie down objects.

We all work together to make sure everyone is safe and taken care of. Kids are off school and playing, we stock up on really good snacks and drinks, and we sit outside a lot before the storm hits. Maybe it's the nervous energy, but we can't seem to do much except visit with neighbors and loved ones while tracking the storm slowly moving toward us. It's like tracking an exceptionally large, slow-moving turtle until it hits.

We really do have hurricane parties. It's more like a circle of chairs in someone's driveway, but a party nonetheless. I know it sounds irresponsible, but we prepare the best we can, then we wait and come together in community. Again, we're far enough inland to do this safely.

Another acceptable change is as everyday as changing up dinner. How many times have you said, "I'm tired of the same ole same ole. Let's try a new recipe or grab a bite out"? This is another example of acceptable change that's often chatted about with a carefree attitude. Dare I say, a welcome change. No one ever complains about a shift in the nightly meal unless it's taco night, of course. Everyone loves taco night. We share recipes, join meal clubs, and still wish for more options. Most people would be excited to try a new dinner idea.

Recently, my husband came home with the same Dove soap our family has used for years, only the container had changed. It had a new built-in pump. Strangely enough, when I went to grab a new soap from the closet, I was genuinely joyful over the new design. My husband chuckled. Later, my teenage daughter called from the shower, "Can you bring soap?!" As teenagers often do. I'm working with her on becoming more in tune with her needs before she needs them. When I got to her bathroom with the new soap, she excitedly said, "Oh! What is this?" Okay, I promise we're not normally this easily amused, but it shows how slight changes can be fun and desirable, even when unexpected. It adds a little something new and fresh to life. It doesn't take much to see the same ole thing in a whole new light.

Obviously, some change can be extremely uncomfortable. A friend's husband recently lost his job after 25 years with the company. He was unemployed for over a year, and when he finally found something, it was in another state. They had to sell their home, their children had to change schools, she had to leave her coaching job, and the community she had grown to love. But guess what? Now they're thriving in their new world!

As humans, we're very adaptable. We just tend to get comfortable until we're forced to make a move. I love the old saying, "When one door closes, a window of opportunity opens." As I mentioned before, sometimes the door needs to completely shut and lock. You must let go 100%—the whole kit and caboodle. Your life has endless possibilities, but you must release the weight you carry. You can't be all things to all people. Sometimes, you have to choose to follow your happiness and your vibration. You don't have to stay where you are. You're not a tree. You can move.

Everything in life can become stale. Life itself can become stale—not that you're unhappy, but maybe you're just a little bored with the routine. Maybe things feel off, and you want something new to make you feel awake and alive. Sometimes, a little shake-up is all you need.

MAKE SPACE FOR CHANGE

I'm not sure which social media platform I saw this on, but it encouraged people to invite change by making room for it. Maybe clear out a drawer or a closet, creating space for something new. It even suggested that if you didn't have time for major spring cleaning, you could simply push all your socks to one side of your sock drawer and invite change.

So that's exactly what I did. I pushed my socks to the side and, while standing alone in my closet, I said aloud, "Universe, I have made room for, and welcome, healthy change in my life." Well, holy moly—did a flood of change come my way! Immediate, hurricane-level change. Some good, some not so good, but everything that shifted caused me to shift. It pushed me to respond and be more engaged in my own life, which ultimately brought a feeling of purpose—and a little bit of panic.

One of the not-so-good changes was that two of our five employees resigned just as two others went on maternity leave. My husband, one of our long-term employees, and I were left to batten down the hatches and make it through the tough stretch of being short-staffed. One of the good changes, though, was that business started picking up, and we received a huge order. Another positive that came out of the challenges is that my husband and I became reengaged with the company. The three of us worked hard, but we had a lot of fun getting our clients' needs met. We ended up having one of the best months the company had seen in years.

Meanwhile, things were changing in my personal life, too. We bought a mountain home with friends and decided to try our hand at the vacation rental business. One of my daughters moved out of state, my son got engaged, and we welcomed a brand-new grandbaby. So many changes!

Do you think all of these changes were just a coincidence, or was I simply more attuned to the natural changes already unfolding in my life? Had my brain been awakened to notice and react to them more consciously—and more powerfully? Did my perspective shift, or did my interactions with those around me change, which set off the ripple of change? Maybe it was the sock drawer. Maybe it was just normal life, or maybe it was me paying more attention. Can you truly call upon change? I believe that, through observation and a willingness to receive, you can invite it.

Checking in with all aspects of your life should be as fluid and regular as checking in with the weather, dinner, or your sock drawer. It's normal to get bored with the everyday routine. However, if you're in perfect flow, you should feel more alive. Your days should feel purposeful and productive. You might even walk with a pep in your step. I'm a firm believer that what and who you are is what and who you attract. You're meant to feel alive and to experience the world around you.

Wouldn't it be nice if there were an app that gave you predictions for the changes about to happen in your life? Today, there's an 80% chance you'll be late due to traffic, a 40% chance you'll be annoyed with your teenage daughter for not doing her chores, and a 30% chance your boss will mention the promotion you've been eying. Wow! If you could get that prediction in the morning, you'd sure be prepared for the day. You could leave early for work, text your daughter to remind her about her chores (maybe offer to take her to see the kittens at the shelter if she gets them done), and even have something clever ready to say to your boss about that promotion. You could be the superhero of your day with that kind of knowledge.

What if I told you that if you're in tune with your own vibration, you might just be able to predict changes before they arrive? If you could train your brain to predict what will happen next and prepare to react quickly with the best outcome, you'd win far more than you lose. Here's a secret: predictions have a lot to do with your gut.

FOLLOW YOUR GUT

Ever feel like you just knew something—good or bad—was coming? We've all had some level of a sixth sense or gut feeling. The goal is to have that all the time, and even be able to control the outcome. How? By getting accustomed to predicting, interpreting the stimuli, and responding accordingly. It takes time, but with practice, it gets easier. Once you become deeply familiar with your vibration, you'll be more in tune with the world around you and how it might affect you.

Remember how your grandmother knew it was going to rain because her knee hurt? Same concept. You learn to make predictions based on how your body feels about the things and vibrations around you. As women, we've all had that creepy feeling when we know we need to get out of a situation. It's about trusting those instincts—the vibrations and energy surrounding you. It's listening to your inner voice and training it to speak more clearly. Nearly every woman has a story on this point. Some are near-misses, while others become stories of survival meant to warn others. The common theme in most of them is the undeniable sense that something isn't right—a gut-wrenching feeling that can't be ignored.

This intuition isn't so much a feeling of fear, which has a distinct sensation in our bodies. It's more a feeling of knowing—a strong, physical sensation that can't be ignored. Learn to trust this valuable resource that lives within you. Learn to feel the good and bad things coming your way, then focus on the movement you take toward or away from them.

Ever notice when you're contemplating buying a certain kind of vehicle, and suddenly, see is that brand of car? Your brain has shifted to notice and recognize that car. It gets rewarded with dopamine—the pleasure chemical—every time it finds that car, so it relentlessly searches for it.

What if you were in constant communication with yourself? What if you could train your brain to notice certain things? What if you were conscious of what you want and what you feel? What if you could seek out what you want? What if you walked with intention throughout your day, rather than reacting to what is happening to you or around you? You're in more control than you realize. You are a soul inside a body, but sometimes the body seems to be on autopilot, and the soul seems to be binge-watching memories from the past, unaware of what's coming and unable to react fast enough.

The key is to get to know yourself. Reconnect with your thoughts and feelings—not just what needs to be done to get through the day, but what could be. Sit with yourself. It might feel unnatural at first, but you need to get to know yourself and what you truly desire.

When I was 10, I didn't know I was an individual yet. I was my parents' child, but as I witnessed things I didn't want to participate in, I found my individualism. I knew what I didn't want, but it took some time to figure out my purpose and what I did want. I remember going to Sunday school and hearing the lessons telling us that we all had a gift and a calling. It took me a long time to find mine. When I couldn't come up with an answer for what I had to offer the world, I felt very uncomfortable. I even felt lost or unworthy. But I kept coming back. I kept asking myself who I am and what my greater purpose was. Keep searching. Your gifts and calling might change over time. Growth can be uncomfortable, but it's worth the discomfort.

When I first tried yoga, I remember feeling so uncomfortable with child's pose and resting pose. Child's pose was physically uncomfortable, and resting pose was mentally uncomfortable. Now, I love both. It takes practice to sit with yourself in quiet. To be with your own thoughts. I remember lying there and thinking, "Well hello there, self," and feeling so silly. Yoga taught me to speak to myself with kindness. It changed everything for me. I wasn't necessarily mean to myself, but I certainly was ignoring me. I had no idea what I wanted or needed. I just did what was expected of me—what others thought I should do or achieve, or even not do or not achieve. I wanted more than what others saw for me, and for too long, I believed them and allowed their perception of me to limit my dreams. I allowed their opinion of my capabilities to dictate my efforts. Once I started believing in myself and the things I thought I could achieve, the better I did for me. Your short- and long-term goals should be in constant thought and awareness. They should be designed to suit you, for you, and by you.

PRACTICE *makes* POSITIVE

Others can only see you from the outside. From the outside, I was nothing special. Just normal. Maybe perceived as a young, dumb girl. Sweet, maybe, cute little girl even, but nothing special. I was completely non-threatening and dismissive to most people for most of my life. But on the inside? On the inside, I was waiting to roar! On the inside, there was nothing timid or boring about me! On the inside, I had dreams of grandeur. I didn't know how to get there. I didn't know if I was even allowed to see myself any other way than the way others saw me. Over time, I learned to be me a little more on the outside too. I learned to listen to my voice and speak louder. I learned not to allow others to dismiss me. I learned my dreams were bigger. I learned to fight for the things I wanted.

Don't let other people's perception of you dictate who you are. Remember, only you can see the inside and what you are truly capable of. You are your biggest advocate. Learn to listen to yourself, to what you want, and who you are. Train your brain to work from the inside out and not the outside in. Train your brain to look for the things you can and want to do. Train by practicing.

Give this exercise a try. Think of something you want right now—something that would make you happy. Something that has nothing to do with money, another person, or worldly success. Nothing to do with anything but you. Think deeply. What gets you really excited about you and the world around you? Maybe things you want to try or experience? Maybe something you already do that you know you don't want to give up—or maybe you want to do more of it. Write them down. Envision them. If you don't know what it is, how can you make it happen? If you don't know what it is, you'll simply default to scrolling. Figure out what you want and what you like. Try to get your brain searching for what you like, just like the car you want to buy.

SEEK WHAT SERVES YOU.

Practice Makes Positive

So far, I've hinted at the concept of practice—in getting to know your vibration and your deeper self, making small changes, and trusting your gut. In this chapter, I make a strong case for making practice a way of living and being. Why? Because I believe practicing positivity is the key to a beautiful life.

Positive thoughts lead to positive actions, which lead to positive outcomes. Some of us are just naturally positive and always seem happy no matter what happens. If positive thoughts lead to happiness, then why not be positive? Being happy is everything, so let's focus on being positive. If you focus on the good stuff, you should be happier.

Think of Dolly Parton. You really cannot find a more positive person than her, yet she grew up facing huge obstacles, including poverty. Dolly was not going to let anything stop her from reaching her dreams. Ever since she was a little girl, she knew what she wanted. She recognized that her vibration was bigger than others'—not in a mean way, but just that her vibration was stronger. And she wasn't going to give up on her vibration just because other people didn't see or understand it.

Once she reached her dreams, she did not let a day go by without expressing her gratitude and giving back to her hometown community. She still touches people in a way no one else can. She always has a kind word to say. She lifts others up.

Another iconic celebrity who seems to embody positivity despite rising above so much tragedy is Oprah. Like Dolly, she also came from poverty, but Oprah also suffered abuse in her youth. Yet, she is so inspirational. She could see past what was happening to her. She is grounded, full of poise and grace. The one thing she seemed to understand early on was that people have different vibrations, and each one needs to stay true to their own beat. She encourages individuality and being just who you are. She always seems to say just the right things, and she, too, encourages others.

Obviously, I don't know either of them personally, but I grew up watching them, modeling them, and seeing a small piece of me in them—a piece I wanted to nourish and grow. I wanted to spread the same joy and love I saw flowing out of them. I loved their vibration. I wanted to learn some of their magic. You can look for things you like in others, things you want to become, and start visualizing and practicing it. Practice what you want to become. Practice who you want to become. Practice makes positive.

Now, I'm clearly no Oprah nor Dolly, but they taught me to shine my tiny light and not let anyone blow it out. We all need mentors and heroes to look up to. We may never grow as large as they have, but we can make big vibrations in our own little worlds.

My favorite thing about these women is, and keep in mind this comes from the eyes of a little girl or even a young woman who looked up to them, they owned their vibration. They knew who they were, what they had to offer, and they didn't let anyone's opinions stop them from doing or being what they wanted. In fact, it seemed they might have even had a little "I'll show you" attitude, and I for sure relate to that!

They owned the good, the bad, and the ugly within them. They knew they were different—maybe even special. They didn't let anyone take that away. It was theirs to keep. They had big dreams. They were poor. They were female. They faced obstacles and challenges. They were told "no" plenty of times. But they kept going. They used every bit of who they were to get where they wanted to go. They didn't just use the good parts; they used all of it. Even the parts they didn't like, because it was still part of their experience. They knew the obstacles they survived and carried with them were a part of what made them. They took the knowledge and lessons from those experiences and used them to better their tomorrow.

I think that's why people love them so much. They're not perfect. Their lives weren't perfect. Their stories weren't perfect. They never pretended to be. They just persevered. They became the heroes of their own story. And that's my favorite kind of story.

TRAIN YOUR BRAIN

Each of us needs to understand our vibration. Life happens around us, but it does not happen to us. It shouldn't change who we are or what we want; it should only change the way we respond. We will evolve, but we shouldn't allow outside forces to limit us. We must choose what we allow in and what we lock out. Our environment can influence us greatly, which is why we need to be mindful of what we surround ourselves with.

The best way to strengthen our connection to our vibration is to train our brain—the right way. Our brains have been trained to see things a certain way since birth. When I was first navigating important relationships, I realized how uncomfortable I was with confrontation. I still don't like yelling or the uncertainty of a fight, whether it's with friends, family, or my spouse. I have to sit with myself and retrain my brain to accept that it's okay for people to be upset sometimes. I must quiet my triggers and find peace in the discomfort. I need to retrain my brain to accept that it's okay for someone to find fault with me or my intentions. This is something I'm still working on. I'm a pleaser to a fault.

Sometimes, you need to retrain your brain to look at food or exercise differently. Sometimes it's about how we handle alcohol consumption or stress. Whatever it is, you've been trained to have automatic responses that may need to be tweaked. You may also need to train your brain to do or see new things you've never done before. And guess what? Retraining takes practice.

In recent years, I've developed the habit of lying in bed for ten extra minutes every morning—not hitting snooze, but spending conscious time with myself. I start by listing what I'm thankful for, then I visualize how I want my day to go. I picture my workout, eating healthy, having amazing interactions with my family, sitting outside with a gentle breeze, and being successful in my workday. I imagine the day going exactly how I'd love it to.

Mornings are also when I focus my mind on thankfulness—thankful for health, family, and safety. Simply being grateful for a home, food, and basic needs can set your day off with a strong, positive perspective. I'm thankful that I woke up and have a healthy body that can get out of bed. Adriene, an online yoga instructor I love, taught me to repeat, "I am thankful for my body; my strong and healthy body." It certainly helps with body image, but more importantly, it puts everything into perspective.

When I was a young, new mom, I discovered a poem that I kept on my refrigerator door. It listed several chores, each followed by a reason to be thankful for it. For example: "I am thankful for this laundry I get to do, because it means we have plenty of clothes to choose from." "I am thankful for the lawn I get to mow, as it means we have a yard to play in." "I am thankful for the job I get to go to, because it means we have a stable income to pay our bills." I loved the simplicity of thankfulness throughout the poem, but what really struck me was the phrase "get to do." It made me realize that not everyone gets to have what we often view as inconveniences or obligations. Clothes, a home, a lawn, and a job—these things can be easily taken for granted.

At night, when I lie down to sleep, I take ten minutes to reflect on the day. I think about what I'm thankful for—whether it's something that happened or something that didn't. I try to keep it positive and focus on the good things. Reflecting on the lessons from the day helps me focus on what I want to carry forward. I avoid letting my mind spiral into regrets

PRACTICE makes POSITIVE

or self-loathing. Everything should stay positive. Be thankful for the lessons, and train your brain to avoid making the same mistakes again.

Your thoughts of thankfulness could be as simple as enjoying nice weather or having a call with an old friend. Maybe it's that you remembered your laptop before you left the house—big win there! Find something that brought you happiness, no matter how small. Reflecting on these moments will train your brain to recognize things to be thankful for moving forward. Your brain might even start seeking out those moments and create opportunities to experience that thankfulness again.

Once your brain knows what you like, it might notice it more—just like when you're thinking of buying a car and suddenly see that make/model everywhere. Your brain will start to see the good stuff and go after it! Training your brain to not only notice what you want but also actively pursue it can become as habitual as grabbing your phone. By focusing on the positive things that happened during your day, you can shift your perspective, making you a happier person—and you might even sleep better! Try it. You may notice a subtle shift in your life. These are small ripples that build over time. Retraining the way you think and feel requires practice, but with daily repetition, a beautiful, powerful habit will develop.

Think about any child you've interacted with. Most children are happy, carefree, and kind, simply happy to just be. But life has a way of hardening us—bills, deadlines, and daily duties often cause us to forget how to prioritize happiness. The good news is, you can retrain your mind to find it again. Reach back and reconnect with that inner child. Talk to her. Maybe she can help you see the good in your day and remind you to be thankful for it.

Improving your thoughts, outlook, and determination is absolutely possible. You can train your brain to look for the good and actively seek it out. Start by setting small goals for yourself and checking your progress. Maybe today, you wake up ten minutes earlier. Or go to bed ten minutes earlier. Maybe you'll read for ten minutes or do yoga for ten minutes. You could spend time with yourself and your thoughts, intentionally keeping them happy and thankful. Or sit with a loved one and just listen for ten minutes. Whatever your first baby step is, start with ten minutes and commit to it every day for at least one month.

I've suggested ten minutes because it's a manageable starting point, an easy commitment. Choose something that speaks to your happiness and promotes your mental and physical health. The goal is to connect better with yourself and your vibration.

If it helps, journal your progress. Or if that's too much, set a daily reminder on your phone to check in with yourself. Notice where you are, how you're feeling, and what would make you happy in that moment—or the moments to come. Learn to recognize what you could do or change to feel better. It may be as simple as turning on some music or stepping outside. But try to make those moments all about you and your thoughts, not about what's happening on social media.

If you don't get an answer right away, that's okay. Keep practicing, and eventually, you will. You can practice during your commute, your lunch break, or before bed. It only takes ten minutes, but it needs to be a daily habit. Once you start trusting yourself, it will become second nature. You'll get to the point where you can almost stop time, check in with yourself, and then respond to situations more mindfully. You will be more in control of your world and your outcomes when you master this practice.

LEARN TO RESPOND VERSUS REACT

We can train our brains to respond instead of react. A reaction is automatic and uncontrolled. A response, on the other hand, is thought out. You take in information, assess the situation, and respond accordingly. By controlling how we respond, we gain more control over what happens next—and that can change everything. Imagine always doing and saying the right thing. How amazing would that be? It just takes slowing down and paying closer attention.

Can you imagine being so in tune with your wants and needs that you notice opportunities sooner? Would you be able to predict obstacles before they arise? Can your brain be trained to see things you never noticed before? Absolutely!

Ever notice how good things always seem to happen to certain people? They seem incredibly lucky! Maybe it's because they've trained their brains to see the good because they're actively looking for it—maybe even expecting it. They're in a constant state of seeking growth through change and mindset, always one step ahead of the forces around them. Being prepared and ready to receive or reject what they need. Yesterday, X was right for me, but today I'm feeling more Y. So, search for Y. Constantly optimizing for happiness teaches your brain to scan for the best thing at any given moment. You can respond, grasp it, and make it yours.

Here's an example: If you know you need to turn right in a mile, your brain is already trained to look for an opening in traffic. What if you applied this to your work environment? What if you were so familiar with your career path and growth opportunities that you could highlight your skills when the chance arises? When an opening appears, you'd spot it first and seize the moment. You'd be actively watching for the right opportunity, knowing what's expected and seeking chances to shine. This is the difference between being on autopilot and being an active participant.

This is why some people always seem to get what they want—they're always open to and actively looking for optimization. They're making small, purposeful moves toward their goals. You can do it too. When we get what makes us happy, we are happy—and happiness attracts happiness! This creates a cycle worth repeating.

PRACTICING RELATIONSHIPS

Getting in tune with our own needs and desires may require checking in with our loved ones first. Our relationship with ourselves and with others both need to be in alignment, and the only way to know if they are is through regular check-ins.

Investing in people and the relationships we have is crucial. There are people we go through life with, and their vibrations must at least be harmonized. Think about musicians—they warm up together, making sure their instruments are in tune. They hum or make vocal sounds to ensure their notes blend. We went to an orchestra concert once, and I was amazed at how one musician would closely watch another. He would mirror her movements, adjusting his playing to weave in and out of hers, while she stayed focused on her own beat. One led, the other supported, and they switched roles depending on the song. They always knew when it was time to take charge and when to support. Especially during up-tempo pieces, they understood how crucial it was for each stroke to be perfectly timed—otherwise, the whole performance would sound off.

This is how you should interact with your people. Sometimes it's your time to shine, sometimes to support, sometimes to lead, and sometimes to follow. These roles need to be discussed and practiced regularly. Honest communication is key—saying what's working and what's not. It may even take trying different approaches and starting from scratch.

Even a professional group like the New York Symphony Orchestra still practices together. They don't just learn a piece, perfect it, and show up for concerts. They rehearse together, constantly adjusting and communicating. They shift lead chairs depending on the song, skill set, and who they're playing with at the time. They adapt to the audience, the acoustics, the weather, and their own physical state, recognizing limitations or abilities that vary each day.

This is exactly how we should approach our relationships. Regular micro adjustments, communication, and observation help keep them in tune.

You need to put in the work to have successful relationships. Be the friend you want to find in others. If you're not invited, try inviting. If you're feeling disconnected, try connecting. Find common ground and build on it. Be selfless with your love and kindness. Avoid judgment and gossip. Love with all you have. When that love comes back to you, it will be so worth it! Make others feel the way you want to feel. Treat them as you want to be treated. If you have a positive thought about someone, share it—even with a simple text. Respect their vibration and see if you can make music together.

A NOTE ABOUT TEXTING

I once heard a radio talk show discuss text communication and how texts can easily be misread or misconstrued. The simple answer was to assume positive intent. Easy enough, right? Just re-read it and interpret it in a friendly, kind way. If you get a text that leaves you wondering about the meaning, read it again and assume positive intent. Even if their words weren't meant kindly, respond with love and kindness. This way, your emotions and vibration stay happy and in alignment, creating your own little bubble. Sometimes, it's best to ignore it. Maybe they just wanted to be heard. No need to react or prove your point—your goal is to stay on your vibration, no matter what they throw your way. There's no need or obligation to catch it.

For example, if your husband sends a text saying, "I see you're running late, I guess I'll start dinner," you might read it and think there's an undertone, possibly tempting you to get defensive. Instead, assume positive intent and respond with, "I really appreciate that, darling. Thank you for being so attentive to our household. This is exactly the help I needed, and maybe we'll even have extra time tonight to start that show you wanted to watch."

This interaction could easily go in two very different directions. Hopefully, a positive response will set the right tone. It takes practice, but shifting to a positive perspective truly changes the outcome over time.

PART OF A HERD

Humans are natural herd animals. We live in neighborhoods, join fraternities and sororities, attend church, marry, and make connections with both people and groups. We have reunions with classmates and families, creating communities wherever we go. Being part of a community gives us pride, purpose, and validation. Without it, one might feel isolated or lonely.

Consider how much we love our sports teams. We're not even playing the game, yet we cheer like we are part of the team. We buy jerseys, sit in the stands through any weather, and talk about the team like it's our own. Why? Because, in some way, it is. It's the hometown team, the team our parents loved, or the little league squad we played for. It's the underdog that made it to the championship. These teams connect us, give us hope, and offer something to look forward to—or cry about. They stir emotions that take us away from the everyday. I've seen grown adults cry over a team's loss, feeling deeply connected to those colors. We host parties around football games, teach our kids to play, and for some of us, we live for football season. It brings a sense of belonging, companionship, and friendly competition—which, of course, leads to some legendary trash talk.

I tease, but the feeling of belonging might just be the most important emotional need we have as humans. We need to feel connected to something bigger, something meaningful. We need to be part of our herd.

On the flip side, the greatest punishment we face is being an outcast or unwanted. We need love and acceptance—it's just how we're wired. But to be the best for others, you must first be the best for yourself. Fill your own needs and desires before you can give to anyone else. Love yourself first, then love others. And remember, this takes constant practice and kindness in your thoughts.

So, discover who you are, what you like and don't like, and then find a few communities to join. You can (and should) have more than one. Check in with those relationships often. Celebrate what you bring to your herd—bring something special that no one else offers. You may be quieter in some groups, and in others, you might lead. Both are necessary and good. Some groups may be temporary, some lifelong.

Make music with the ones who will be in your life for the long haul. Love them for all that they are and all they bring. Give them space, and take space when needed. Learn when to be quiet and when to play loud. This will be a dance you do forever—practice it again and again.

LIVING IN A BUBBLE

My entire life, I've been told I live in a bubble. "I wish I could live inside your head for a day," some have said—though not always kindly. I've even been told my reality is off, or that I'm too happy. Too happy? If that's a problem, I don't want to be right! Maybe I've trained my brain to find the positive in things, but I wouldn't want it any other way. I hope my bubble never bursts.

I don't want to live a life that doesn't feel worth living. If I didn't like something in my life, I'd change it. I'd find a way to make it better or more comfortable, at least until I could find a way out. So, I love my life. I love my people. I love my neighborhood. I love my 8-year-old car. I love love itself—and I will continue to be this way. Love the people and things in your life every day.

I like to think I work to live, rather than live to work. When something feels off, I find something new. Life isn't always perfect, but if it's really bad, get up and walk away. Take a new path and see if the world around you changes for the better. Even if what you're leaving behind seems like where you should stay, find a new herd! Find a new path! Find a new perspective!

Most importantly, don't let others' interpretation of your life influence you. People can say the meanest things. Don't let that affect your emotions, happiness, or decisions. Your vibration is yours alone. This is your life, and you must stay in control of what you allow in. It's meant only for you. No one else can or will fully understand it—and they're not meant to. Protect it, appreciate it, and nourish it. Learn to love it, because it's what makes you, you.

When someone questions your vibration, instead of doubting it yourself, just play it louder! Dance to it like no one is watching! After all, it's your bubble!

BRACE YOURSELF

After much practice, once you know what you want and are ready to make a change, brace yourself. People naturally question what's different—until it becomes greatness. Then, they celebrate it and may even covet it. Remember, difference can become greatness.

Expect pushback from those around you. You're changing, evolving, and doing things they don't expect. This can make your loved ones nervous—for you, for the outcome, or even because they worry you might outgrow them.

Small adjustments over time are usually best, but sometimes something inside you just needs to come out. Talk to those around you. Set goals, timelines, agreements, and arrangements. Communication is key. Know what you want, and plan for it. Confidence is incredibly attractive, but arrogance is not. Stay in the sweet spot, leaning more toward the beautiful side.

Sometimes, you need a bit of arrogance to find confidence, but always be kind. A little pep talk in the mirror is fine—but kindness to others is nonnegotiable.

Sometimes, when you try to change for the better, your relationships might face challenges. Loved ones might not understand why you want to stop doing something you've always done, or they might feel like you're distancing yourself. They likely enjoyed things the way they were, or they enjoy the habit you're trying to limit.

For example, if you're trying to cut back on drinking during the week, your friends might give you a hard time at your regular Wine Down Wednesday. You may even need to avoid going to avoid the pressure to conform. The best approach is to communicate your vision and goals. Let them know what you're working toward and ask for their support when you order a mocktail.

You could say, "I know we always had fun at Wine Down Wednesday, but I've set some new goals for myself and would appreciate your encouragement. Maybe we could have a weekly lunch instead and start a new way of connecting?"

A good friend will appreciate your intentions and be excited to join you in this new direction.

The same can happen when you want to try new things. Those closest to you might question why you're not happy with the old ways. They may be comfortable with things as they are and don't want you to want more. Again, communication is key. Reassure them that you're not leaving them behind or giving up what you love together; you simply want to experience new things and evolve alongside them.

For example, if you want to try pickleball but your weekly run with your running partner conflicts with the schedule, suggest a new time to run, invite them to pickleball, or simply acknowledge that you need a change. You're allowed to change, and sometimes what you once loved no longer fits. It doesn't mean you don't care about the person—it just means the song is over. Honest communication is the best approach.

Life can throw curveballs. We may outgrow something or someone due to a death, job loss, or move. When that happens, relationships may come to an end. Be cautious about making too many changes too quickly, as you still have to navigate the ripples of those changes.

During times of change, it's important to have support. An ending can hurt, but it also marks the start of something new. Allow yourself to grieve and lean on others for love and support. Maybe you need a neighbor to watch your child while you take a class or ask your teenager to make dinner while you work late. It's okay to ask for help—and guess what? Asking takes practice. Change is uncomfortable for everyone, so do what you can to make it easier.

LETTING GO

The best thing about being young is the endless possibilities ahead of you. You haven't yet built up memories or regrets. That day will come—and that's okay. It's how we learn, figure out what we want, and train our brains to seek out what we enjoy.

As we move through life, regrets and "what-ifs" will tug at our hearts. We'll make mistakes. You might be the person who hurts someone, or you might be the one who gets hurt. The key is to let go and keep looking forward. Financial or emotional setbacks can sting, but they're just moments in time. With the knowledge gained, you can move forward and use it to make better choices in the future.

Sometimes, what once was can no longer be. There are always more and better things ahead. The best is yet to come. I believe our vibration is like music, while life is a journey—a river. There are rapids, waterfalls, and peaceful pools of beauty. Enjoy each stage, but remember none of them are meant to last forever. What's around the bend will always be a mystery. The goal is to choose what brings you peace and joy as much as possible. As our paths change, we naturally change too—our wants, perceptions, and experiences evolve.

Maybe something that needs to end just does, and you need time to mourn. It's okay to feel sorrow and weakness. Depending on the loss, it may take time to process the grief. Just be mindful not to stay stuck in a low place. When it's the right time for you, take time to think through your choices, make sure you have support, and walk toward your next step with confidence.

Sometimes, we must not only shut a door but lock it and even barricade it before we can see the window of opportunity open. We have to let go of one thing to see the path to the next. It's hard to fully let go of something we once loved. As long as we're holding on, even just a little, we stay stuck. If it's no longer meant to be, you probably already know it; it's just painful or scary to admit, especially when thinking of life without it.

We're here for the ride—the journey, the ups and downs, the waterfalls, and the rapids. Enjoy the scenery, but know your vibe and let the waters carry you until it's time to choose the next stream. Don't become a mindless floater, but take chances and allow yourself breaks along the way.

MAKING RIPPLES

We create ripples in our vibrations from day one through conscious, deliberate actions. Often, we feel those ripples circling back to us much later—years and even decades of ripples still finding their way back. When they do, we either love what's coming or feel extremely uncomfortable with it. If we've made a series of small, bad decisions, life might feel like a mess, and things may begin to stir around us. If we've made mostly good decisions, we might feel pretty good about where we are.

Most of us make both good and bad ripples along the way, which can make our waters feel like a washing machine. This mix can make it seem like the waterway is blocked or unclear. Maybe a big boulder stands in the way, or we can't see what swims below the surface.

The good news is we can always start over. We can even dive into a whole new body of water. Flush the pipes. The sad news is we may hurt others, ourselves, or our situation. We leave room for regret to seep in. This is why we must think things through, communicate openly and honestly with ourselves and our loved ones, and continue the practice of daily check-ins. A bigger disruption might push us out of alignment, but honesty is always best. No one can fault you for taking responsibility for your actions and the ripples they cause, especially if you're working to set the course right again.

For me, when I divorced my first husband, I didn't just change my family dynamic—I also changed our geography. My children had new schools, new friends, and a new father figure almost overnight. It took me a long time to come to this decision, but once I made up my mind, I moved quickly. To the outside world and my family, it seemed to come out of nowhere. But to me, it was something I had agonized over for over a year. At the time, I didn't like the direction my life was going, so I made giant leaps with confidence and speed, not fully understanding the destruction I was creating along the way.

With every fresh start, you leave behind an abandoned space—one that's no longer yours to tend to. Ripples are made in that space. Once you're gone, you can't change what happens there, only how you handle the ripples when they eventually return to you.

We can start fresh, but it requires recognizing what we need, what we're giving, and what we're willing to receive. It also requires forgiveness—for ourselves and others. You don't want to drag mud into your new, clear water. There will be hurts to heal. The best decisions you can make for yourself might unintentionally cause pain for others. You'll have to decide if that pain is worth it. However, you might not see the damage you cause until you're on the other side.

When you're building your life and your relationships, it's important to be mindful of who you let in and who you associate with. The people you choose will influence your vibration, and you'll change theirs. Think about the old sayings: "You are what you eat" or "You become who you hang out with." You become more vulnerable to the energy of those you allow into your life. That's why it's important to be selective. Associate with people you want to emulate.

The ones we love most are the ones who see us at our most vulnerable, and they can greatly influence our thoughts, actions, and outcomes. We bounce ideas off them, ask questions, and make plans for the future with them. We become each other's counselors. So, be selective about who you let in and what level of influence you give them.

Beware of the myth that you can change someone for the better. We sometimes stay stuck with the wrong people because we fear what we would be without them. We give others too much power over our vibration, thinking they play the game better. But if you keep giving your vibration away, you'll eventually lose your own voice and not know who you are anymore. This can apply to a best friend, spouse, coworker, or even a parent.

I'm not saying to get rid of an important relationship, but make sure they're good for you and only let in what serves you. Maybe some boundaries need to be set. Maybe time needs to be limited for a while. Maybe the routine needs to change.

REACTIONS CAUSE RIPPLES

It amazes me how we each react differently to the same situation. A few friends of mine were about 10 car lengths from a really bad accident. They were far enough back that they couldn't see what was going on, but they knew people were turning off their cars and preparing to wait for a while. My friends rolled down the windows, enjoyed some fresh air, turned off the car, and decided to just chat while they waited for things to clear.

After some time, they realized a life flight helicopter was circling. This was a bad one. My friends felt so bad for whomever was hurt, praying for them and their families. They felt empathy for those involved and a thankfulness for their own health. There was also a sense of relief that they were not the ones 10 car lengths up.

As time passed, they noticed some people getting out of their cars. One woman was fully taking advantage of the moment, picking flowers and taking pictures of nature, while others were talking and pacing between cars. Once the ambulance zoomed by, delivering the injured person to the helicopter that had landed behind them, one gentleman started yelling, "What is the hold-up now?! Things should start moving now that the person has been relocated!" He was obviously agitated. Everyone was astounded by his reaction. He seemed so out of place. Heartless.

His reaction was caused by more than just this current window of time and place. He couldn't see past his own needs and sense of urgency. He had yet to learn the valuable lesson of responding to situations rather than reacting to them. He was not in control of his mind, his vibration, his response, or his outcome. Everyone in this situation was reacting to the same stimuli in their own unique way and from different perspectives. Their reactions were likely shaped by where they were headed next in life. No one was in control, and no one could change the experience. But each person could choose how they responded to the moment and what they did with the time given to them.

Most people don't even know who they are or what they want until later in life. Maybe it's when those ripples in our vibrations start coming back to us, either making us happy or uncomfortable enough to want change. Just learn to be in tune with yourself and stay open to opportunities as they arise. Whatever you do, it only needs to make sense to you. You must find your happiness on your own. No one will care about the outcome more than you. You are the only one who needs to be happy with the ripples you make and the vibration you exude. You are the only person who will be with you from beginning to end. You have been awarded the solo performance of your lifetime. You are the creator and the recipient. I like that. You are the creator and the recipient. Create what you love, and you will be happy.

WHEN THINGS FEEL OFF, ADJUST.

Lessons Learned

EVERYTHING PICKS UP ON YOUR VIBRATIONS

When you're not happy, everything around you picks up on it. You send out small frequencies into the air that touch everything around you. Whether happy or toxic, your vibrations are felt without you even noticing. Everything will respond to your energy, either thriving or deteriorating, often without anyone noticing at first. Both your verbal and nonverbal cues are felt, and people will adjust to you, even on the smallest scale. Of course, some will blossom in the worst environments, while others may struggle in the best.

Have you ever noticed how some people learn perseverance in the worst situations, while others crumble? At the same time, someone born with privilege might fall while others use that privilege as a springboard? Your environment is important, but how you respond to it is even more so. You're constantly receiving and sending vibrations into the world, responding at the most basic level.

Your message can be simple—a big sigh, a raised eyebrow, or looking down instead of making eye contact. You might appear bothered, rushed, distracted, or uninterested. On the other hand, you might seem overly eager or too interested. Either way, you're communicating. Your vibration is speaking. Even when you try to hide your feelings, put on a smile, and act like everything's fine, everyone and everything around you knows it's not

53

the case. The universe knows, your children know, your coworkers know— even strangers subconsciously pick up on your vibration. Everything that has life and breath can feel it on some level. No matter how hard you try to mask it, you can't get away with it. You're only building a house of cards that will eventually crumble.

Ever notice how, when you see a loved one, the first thing you say is, "What's wrong?" You can just feel it. You can see it on their face and in their actions, even when they don't know they're expressing it. My mom was great at reading me—better than anyone I've ever met. It made me feel both safe and terrified, all at once. Even toward the end, I could call her, and the moment she heard my voice, she would just say, "What's wrong?"

Most of her life, my mom was the most loving and caring person I'd ever met—selfless and giving. And what a hoot! She was the life of any party, always with a good story to tell. In the end, she developed some form of dementia, and well, it was just hard. Sometimes, she was the reason my vibration was off. She was the one thing I couldn't fix, fill, or please. There were moments when calling her felt like an obligation because she was so grumpy. But when she'd ask what was wrong, I'd simply cry. I never told her it was her declining health that made me sad. She'd just listen and say, "Oh baby, I'm so sorry." In those moments, I felt so connected to her again. I had my mom back. Even though she never knew what had made me cry, she'd be there with me through the sadness, reassuring me everything would be okay.

Moving her into a community home in February 2020 for socialization turned out to be a social prison. Due to the Covid outbreak, she was confined to her room for seven months. This environment changed her. So much of our environment molds and affects our lives. Like plants, we either thrive in our environment or wilt away. If the environment is confining or toxic, we feel it. It wears on us and changes us.

Sometimes, it's the other living things in our environment that act as a barometer for us. Plants and children will show distinct signs when they're placed in an unhealthy environment. A friend of mine owns a Pilates studio I frequent often. She had several plants in the studio that seemed to struggle. Not enough to die, but enough to look sick and wilted.

She was also in a relationship that just didn't seem right. They'd been together for two years but had come to a wall. They loved each other, but they weren't ready to take the next step together. Not enough to die, but enough to look sick and wilted for a spell. They eventually broke up, and she dated a few others for about a year.

She and her plants were fine, but they weren't flourishing. She read some self-help books and set clear standards for what she wanted in her next relationship. If she went on a date and the person didn't meet her standards, she simply wouldn't see them again. Just like that. She might have liked them, even been attracted to them, but if they didn't align with the criteria she knew would lead her to the next levels of love, she wouldn't waste her time or theirs. She wasn't going to let anyone back in who she couldn't see building a life with. I'm not talking about money—she has her own—but things like the age of children, stage of divorce, outlook on life, and hobbies.

She no longer wanted to waste time allowing the wrong people into her world. In her mind, she had already spent enough time with the wrong ones. So, she set goals for herself and checked in daily to ensure she was making micro movements in the right direction toward the future she wanted.

Now, she's married to the adventurous, happy, wonderful partner she always wanted. Their love of travel, ocean life, and desire for growth make them a strong match. And for me, it's her plants! All of them are thriving—thriving! I'm telling you, the things around you feel your vibration, and when it's off, nothing will do well. You are creating an environment that others feel and react to on the smallest level, but it's there, and it can change everything.

That's why it can feel like no matter what you do, or how hard you try to make something work, it just won't. Not until you're aligned with your own vibration. I can't emphasize this enough: make time and space to learn who you are and what you want. You're only doing good for yourself and those around you when you're in proper vibration. Live in your vibration. You and everyone you love will be better for it.

Sometimes we crave change to the point of destruction. We get so tired of the mundane routine that we fantasize about what our life could be if we had that car, that job, or that partner. "My life would be better if..."

These are the thoughts and actions we must avoid. While it's important to be mindful of your happiness and make small adjustments, that doesn't mean justifying hurting those around you or creating a fantasy life. When the changes you're considering challenge your moral compass, it's best to avoid them. Desire for change doesn't mean destroying what you've built. Instead, make healthy changes that cause no harm.

The good news is, if you check in with yourself and your loved ones regularly, these adjustments can happen naturally, almost daily, without the need for a big, disruptive change. My grandmother used to say, "Don't throw the baby out with the bathwater." You don't have to walk away from the people you love to find happiness. Small getaways, special moments, a shift in perspective, and open conversations can make all the difference. Happiness and fulfillment come from within, not from others.

Life isn't meant to be perfect every day. Some days are just meant to be filler. In a perfect world, every day would be magical—like the best day ever, every day. I struggle with those simple, uneventful days. But the truth is, you need the boring days to make the good ones special.

I've learned that I like to run at a level ten whenever I can—living life at full speed. However, most people can't—or don't want to—keep up with that pace every day. So I've come to accept the filler days, respecting my loved ones' quieter vibrations and not exhausting them. Protect your relationships. The journey is more rewarding when shared with others.

Life is about anchoring yourself to someone, no matter what changes. But it starts with anchoring yourself to your own vibration. Be true to who you are and stay true to your values. If you betray those core values, you might end up in a place of self-loathing.

If you find yourself lost in a relationship and don't recognize who you've become, take small steps back to your authentic self. Don't turn your world upside down, just acknowledge the disconnect and listen to your inner voice. Reconnect with the love that once was, and may still be. Sometimes, letting life move under you while you stay still is the best approach. Get to know yourself before making too many changes.

At one point in my marriage, when we still had all five kids at home, my husband and I found ourselves sitting in the car in our garage. Okay, it was our new minivan... which eventually became one of my favorite vehicles, though I originally called her Tiffany just to avoid saying "the minivan." But I digress. We were in the garage (engine off), having stumbled upon a spot where we could finish a conversation without the kids finding us. It became our secret place, and we still laugh about it today.

It doesn't take money or much time to change things up a little. Connections are what truly make a difference. Small changes add up over time, keeping us in check with ourselves and each other. Finding time alone in a healthy way can help too. Join a Bible study, a book club, or simply spend time in your backyard reading. Just take yourself out of the daily rut.

This action alone can shift the energy between two people. But remember, this isn't meant to be a silent treatment—just space to breathe. Then, when you reconnect, make eye contact and smile. Do this again and again. Practice makes positive.

BEWARE THE LOOP

Try not to re-live the same lessons over and over. If you're stuck in a loop you can't escape, it's usually because you're doing the same things, expecting different results. That's the definition of insanity, my friends.

One of my friend's children was struggling in math. Last semester, she missed a math test and retook it the next day. But her teacher never entered the score, and as the semester was nearing its end, she was facing a zero instead of the make-up test score. She felt the teacher wasn't listening or caring, so she went to an aide who helped get the score entered just in time.

Keep in mind, this wasn't the only reason she was struggling in math, but she's working on that lesson too. Fast forward to the next semester, when a math test was scheduled for a half-day. This is when kids only go to school for half the day, and teachers use the other half for planning. Of course, this often makes kids want to take a mental health day to sleep in instead of going to school. Most teachers don't schedule much on those half-days—maybe in hopes of having more time to plan, I don't know.

But this particular math teacher scheduled a test, and this particular student was pretty upset about it. She thought about taking the test the next day as a make-up. Trust me, I get it! But knowing what happened the previous semester, I asked why she would want to risk going through that same painful experience again. Why re-live that lesson? It might be easier, I suggested, to go to school—even if it's just for math—and take the test to ensure her grade gets entered correctly.

I was happy to learn that she did go to school and take the quick 5-question math test. I believe this saved her from a lot of potential grief. Most importantly, it kept her in charge of her own outcome. Had she missed the test, she would have allowed the situation to control her emotions. I know she felt powerless and frustrated, but I'm glad she didn't risk reliving those feelings. The lesson she learned was simple: do the thing you might not want to do the first time around, instead of letting it resurface later, more complicated than before.

You can't control every situation, but you can control how you respond. The sooner you learn to respond rather than react, the more in control of your life you will be. When things aren't vibing with you or going your way, there are things you can do to adjust. The goal is to accommodate your own needs, rather than expecting others to adjust to fill them. Responding takes capital "P" practice.

Recognize that when something bothers you, it's you who needs to make the adjustment first. This loop can be tough to break, especially if you're used to reacting from a victim mentality, which might stem from emotional trauma or baggage. To break the cycle, start by finding something you can adjust that's within your control. If you can fix things without affecting anyone else, that's ideal.

However, if it's something you can't fix on your own, approach it with kindness and ask the other person to accommodate. Explain your situation calmly and let them know how you attempted to make changes on your end first. Most of the time, the other person has no idea you're being affected. I promise, the world is not out to get you. Most people are just going through their own lives, not giving much thought to yours. No offense—I'm not saying they don't like you, but they're probably busy trying to remember what they need at the grocery store. The sooner you accept this, the happier you'll be.

Sometimes, no matter what you do, you can't change the experience. Sometimes, you just need to accept it and change the way you respond. The lesson here is to accept what you can't change, change what you can on your own, or speak kindly to someone who can help make the change. Sometimes, you just have to let it go.

BEWARE THE GIFT OF CONTROL

One of my best friend's mantras is, "Peace begins with me." This is absolutely true. We create so much unnecessary drama in our minds. Check in with yourself and see if you can calm your thoughts before anything else.

The greatest gift you can give yourself is control over your life—your perspective, your emotions, and what you choose to make your obligations. Let me repeat that: what you CHOOSE to make your obligations. It's important you absorb this.

You have a choice in what you make an obligation for yourself and for others. Of course, small children are an exception, but once they are old enough, the same principle applies. Doing everything for your loved ones can be harmful for everyone, but it can especially be detrimental for you. Make wise decisions and ensure you're not dimming their light by doing things for them.

If you're the one who swoops in and does it all, life will become overwhelming—and you'll be undermining your loved ones' abilities. Children, especially in elementary school, thrive when given responsibilities. Roles like line leader, door holder, and messenger are prized positions in the classroom. Introducing small responsibilities at home can also give children a sense of pride. Chore charts, with rewards at the end of the week, can be very effective.

Doing too much for your children robs them of their independence and burdens you with too much responsibility. I believe that giving children a sense of responsibility and autonomy in your home instills pride and independence. Even teenagers can gain valuable life lessons by taking on responsibilities. Allowing them to practice adulthood while living with you builds confidence and gives them the knowledge they'll need when you're not around.

When my oldest daughter turned sixteen, she paid half for her car, and we paid the other half. She combined birthday and Christmas money along with some babysitting earnings. Even with our match, she couldn't afford much. Some of her friends were gifted high-end cars, while she had to work hard for a clunker. She didn't love this at the time, but I told her she would eventually. I explained that someday, she would be able to buy a nice car on her own, and that day would be one of the best in her life because she'd earned it herself. She paid her own insurance, gas, and spending money, and had to save for maintenance as well. She learned how to manage her finances and budget wisely.

Fast forward to after college, when she was giving financial advice to a friend who had overpaid for a car she couldn't afford. The friend was six months away from paying off the loan, but was thinking about letting the car be repossessed because she could no longer afford the payments. Six months away from clearing a five-year loan! It would ruin her credit and leave her without a car. My daughter called me that night to thank us for teaching her how finances work. She was able to help her friend avoid making a costly mistake. That same year, my daughter bought a really nice car herself, putting a large down payment and shopping around for the best interest rates. It was, indeed, a wonderful day in her life.

Allowing her to suffer a little during the learning process was difficult, but it was worth it in the end. All of my kids have done the same and now have a strong understanding of how finances work.

A friend's daughter was moving out on her own for the first time, and my friend helped her buy some furniture—but not the whole set. She bought the bed frame, mattress, and headboard, but not the dresser or nightstands. A month or two later, she offered to help her daughter complete the room. To her surprise, her daughter bought some used furniture, painted it, and changed the hardware. She sent my friend pictures of the work she was so proud of completing. If my friend had bought her the entire set from the start, not only would it have caused temporary financial hardship for her, but it would have also robbed her daughter of this creative moment of self-fulfillment.

The lesson here is to give your children room to try things on their own. Allow them the time and space to figure it out before you come to their rescue. It might be good for both of you!

What happens if you do too much for your loved ones? Does it rob them of their need to feel productive and valued? Everyone needs to feel valued and productive. If you jump in, does it suggest that you think you can do it better than they can? What does that do to their vibration? Are you exhausted because you're spread too thin or spent too much? What does that do to your vibration?

When you're in alignment with yourself, you're not relying on others for happiness or validation. You don't wait for it to come from the outside—you should be the one in charge of making the changes you need each day to feel fulfilled. You can't wait for others to read your mind. They never will.

Someone once told me, "Other people's failure to plan should not create an emergency for you." You can and should want to help, but in a way that doesn't cause you distress or take away from their successes. That scenario works both ways. Don't expect others to react to your life emergencies with the same level of urgency. If they want to help, great, but you can't get upset if they only wish you well from afar. They might have their own set of mini-emergencies they're trying to solve.

THE GIFT OF ALREADY KNOWING

Sometimes, all you need to do something amazing is permission. Just for someone to simply say, "You can do it." But at the same time, all it takes is someone to say, "That's dumb," or "Are you crazy?" to make you question yourself. This is exactly why we need to live in our own vibration and not take others' opinions too much to heart. You need to be the ultimate decision-maker on whether you can do something or not. You are the driver. This is your rodeo. Whatever mantra you need, make it yours. Listen to your internal voice. That's the only voice you need to trust. Make it a priority to listen to it.

We also need to surround ourselves with the right people. The reason therapists are good at what they do is they rarely tell you what to do. Instead, they ask questions to help you make the decision on your own. They guide you to your own thoughts, giving you the confidence to come to your own conclusions. The answers are already inside of you. Search for them there. This is your life.

Good friends know your background and the behind-the-scenes. They might point out the challenges you faced in the past or the way you felt the last time you made a similar decision. But good friends will support whatever you decide. They will also grow tired of watching you make the same mistakes over and over. So, be sure to notice if they pull back from discussions you keep rehashing. It's probably a sign that you're stuck in a loop.

It's really the naysayers you want to avoid—the ones who may be slightly jealous, bitter, or just fearful. Don't let their emotions cloud your own. Helpful friends will assist you by working through all angles of a decision, rather than pushing you down a one-way street. It doesn't mean they don't care for you; they just may not see all the pathways as clearly as you can. It's okay to listen to their reasoning, but make sure the ultimate decision is yours.

There's some level of wanting to be the best in all of us. A little competition is natural. It doesn't mean we're not happy for our friends, neighbors, and family, but there's always that little voice of, "Why didn't I think of that?" or "Why would you risk so much?" We each have our own level of risk tolerance, confidence, and luck that shapes our destiny. You know what you have in the tank. Trust yourself. Believe in yourself. Wait until you're ready, and then—boom!

For me, I've always felt a responsibility to do all I can with this life I've been given. I've never been someone who could live someone else's dream or not give my hardest effort toward what I want. Maybe that's why my second-grade self never fully got her wish to be a stay-at-home mom and wife to... well, if I'm being honest, to the President of the United States. I mean the president in my hypothetical second-grade dreams, not the ones in office in recent years. I just wanted the guy I liked to become president so I could be the First Lady. The truth is out. I absolutely had a conversation with my husband when we were young and first dating about him running for office. He wasn't interested, but thankfully, I married him anyway. At the time, I thought he was the only one who could do all the things and be the one. I was in my self-doubt era.

But now, I feel the need to make my own mark—to stand on my own two feet and achieve my own independent happiness. This doesn't necessarily translate to financial or outward success, but to my own internal vibration. My personal reflection of my life and how I want to live it. Am I being the best wife, mother, friend, employee, and employer? Am

I being all that I can be for myself today? Am I spending time with my creative side? Am I making myself proud in my interactions? Am I making the world a better place, even in my small existence? Am I exercising and eating healthy? Am I continuing to learn and grow, and setting new goals for myself? Do I feel fulfilled?

My dad used to quote Shakespeare, "Victoria, to thine own self be true." Lots of people live by that, but I first heard it from Dad. Not that he taught me not to care for others' feelings, but he taught me to be true to my dreams, passions, and vibration. We are given one life to do anything we want, and we shouldn't wait for someone to give us permission to live it. We should never, ever let someone stop us from living our passions based on their opinions. I believe we have one purpose: to live OUR best life, whatever that looks like to us.

EXPLORING YOU

Creativity is something I never thought I had. Seriously—not even on the tip of my little pinky finger. I was never the best artist in elementary school, the best dancer in high school, or the best visionary in college. I still question it. But one day, someone told me I should explore my creative side. (There's that permission thing again.) I thought, I don't have one of those. But the more I played around with it, the more it came out.

Now, whether it's any good to the outside world is yet to be determined. But you know what it is good for? My vibration! I feel alive writing this book. I just hit my 10,000-word mark—the first goal I set for myself—and it feels AMAZING. Even if it's just for me. Even if it turns out to be a glorified journal. I've decided to try something new, and I'm in love with the fit.

This is why daily check-ins matter. Why trying new things matters. Why chasing your happiness matters. For no other reason than it feels good to you. And that's all that should matter.

Get out of your routine and stretch yourself beyond your wildest imagination. We are such amazing, beautiful creations. God, the Universe—whatever you call it—wants more for us. I call Him God, but do what works for you. He wants us to experience life, not just live in routine.

Do this for you. Not for fame, not for money—just for your life. For your happiness. So that when you lay down at night, you can think to yourself, Today was a good day.

We have a friend who's 75 and a professor at a university. We recently asked him if he had any plans to retire. He said, "Yeah, in 10 years."

A bit taken aback, we responded, "At 85?"

He shrugged. "Why stop early? I enjoy what I do. My dean says I'm doing a respectable job. The students give me great reviews. I love my days, so why stop?"

Boy, is he living his vibration! I don't think I've ever met anyone more in tune. He plane-glides. He has a sailboat. I see him walking everywhere. He's always well-dressed, always willing to help, always quick with a joke. He's funny, handy, and has the thickest head of hair I've ever seen. He doesn't let anyone dictate his path, his course, or his worth. He doesn't wait for permission, and he doesn't let anyone tell him he can't do something. If someone doesn't like it, he simply shrugs and moves on. He laughs at himself. He cracks jokes about things everyone else is afraid to say aloud. It's great. He's great.

One thing he does not do? Nothing.

So often, we feel the need to decompress. We tell ourselves we need time to relax, to do nothing. And that's okay—to a point. I'm not saying you shouldn't have downtime, but break out of the habit of filling it with things that don't actually bring you happiness. TV can be a trap that eats up an entire Saturday. Hours go by, and you've missed a beautiful day.

True me time should fuel your soul. It should be something you can't wait to do again—something that excites you, makes you feel unique, creative, alive. It should bring you purpose and joy.

So get out of your routine. Try something new. Read a book, hike a new trail, take up painting, photography, or even needlepoint. See how it feels. Take your time, but discover yourself.

Because when you watch TV, you're just watching other people pretend to live.

GO DO IT YOURSELF. LIVE!

Big Dreams, Small Lives

WHAT IF I FAIL?

Go back in time with me for a moment—back to second grade. Picture yourself sitting at your desk in a classroom full of kids. Your teacher stands at the chalkboard, writing down answers as each student shares what they want to be when they grow up. Now it's your turn. She looks at you and smiles.

"What do you want to be when you grow up?"

What's your answer?

In that moment, did you believe you could become what you said? Most of us did. Whether it was an astronaut, a ballerina, or a famous baseball player, we all believed our dreams were within reach—we just had to claim them.

So what happened?

My adult kids have given me a little grief about this. Apparently, I led them to believe they could be anything they wanted, and they thought it would be easier than it actually was. What changed along the way? What made it so hard?

For many of us, life simply takes over. We fall in love, get married, and before we know it, our dreams take a backseat to carpools and dance recitals. Maybe our skillset doesn't quite align with our childhood fantasies. For me, neuropsychology turned out to be a lot more complicated than I could handle—but it's still my favorite class I ever took.

We leave home fueled by passion and ideals, determined to do things our way, to be the best version of ourselves. We're going to climb higher, push further, and take on the world.

But somewhere along the way, we lose momentum. Life beats us down a little. Our passions start to feel exhausting. And eventually, we give in.

We become disenchanted.

Always hold on to at least a small piece of ourselves and our dreams. Maybe you can't be an astronaut, but you can study the stars. Maybe you won't be a ballerina, but you can take a Zumba class. Maybe you won't be a famous baseball player, but you can snag season tickets and cheer on the local team. Maybe becoming a neurophysiologist is out of reach, but you can write an inspirational book that touches someone's life.

It's about creating joyful moments in the everyday and making small adjustments as you evolve. You have to be your own biggest advocate—no one understands what fuels you better than you do. Practice finding your vibration.

Now, what if you could make decisions without worrying about the consequences? I don't mean jumping off a building and hoping you don't hit the ground. But what if, for example, you applied for a job without obsessing over the outcome? Without worrying about not getting it—or worse, getting it and everything that comes with it?

Can I handle it? What if it takes time away from home responsibilities? What if I have to relocate? What if I can't pay my bills while transitioning to a new career? What if they believe in me... and I let them down?

Maybe it's safer to stay put, to stick to what I know, even if it leaves me unfulfilled. It's fine. I'm fine.

But you're not fine.

The endless what ifs are what paralyze most people—not just from change, but from greatness. But what if we didn't worry so much? What if we focused on what feels right today, what excites us in this moment?

Now, I'm not saying abandon all responsibility and lounge on the beach every day just because it sounds appealing. Don't make reckless choices that lead to regret. But what if you opened a little shop by the beach? What if you started a paddleboard rental company so you could be near the ocean every day—if that's what truly lights you up?

I know what you're thinking: I can't do that. I don't even know where to begin. And WHAT IF I FAIL?

That's always the question that stops people in their tracks. What if I fail?

I get it. But what if you don't fail? What if you thrive? What if you wake up happy, fulfilled, and truly living? What sacrifices are you willing to make to see your dreams come true? What small change can you make today to create hope for a better tomorrow?

Real change often requires real sacrifice. And you have to accept the possibility that you might fail. Be okay with losing what you're willing to risk. Be okay with the time and effort it might cost you.

I remember standing at a fork in the road, struggling with a decision. A dear friend gave me a single piece of advice, and in that moment, I knew exactly what to do. He said:

"There is no right answer, but if you follow your heart and fail, your heart will be happy you tried. Your heart and mind will always be at peace if you try. But if you don't, they'll always question what might have been. That unanswered 'what if' can be hard to live with."

I've carried those words with me ever since. Will I spend my life wondering what could have been, or will I give it my best shot, knowing there's a chance I might fail? I'd rather take the risk.

Of course, sometimes pursuing a dream requires financial breathing room. Living paycheck to paycheck makes it nearly impossible to think beyond the next bill, the next shift, the next day. It traps you in survival mode, where there's little room for anything more. And that's a hard place to find your vibration.

If you have some financial freedom, you can start to visualize your dream and map out a way to achieve it.

For example, if your dream is to open a little shop by the ocean, maybe you start by working at one. Maybe you downsize for a year or two—rent a room instead of your own place, or rent out a room in your home for extra income. Maybe you take on a second job and stick to a strict budget. It might be uncomfortable, but with a clear timeline, you can do just about anything.

If you work two jobs for two years and save this much, then with this much, you can take the next step—whatever that may be. Put yourself in the environment you want to be in. Set goals, establish a timeline, and take intentional steps forward. That's how you gain the knowledge and experience necessary to reach your dreams.

Communicate with the important people in your life. Define your goals, set realistic timelines, and establish boundaries that work for everyone involved.

And if you don't know what your dream is yet? Take the time to sit with yourself and figure it out. Maybe this phase of your life requires your focus elsewhere. Maybe your window isn't open yet. Maybe you can't quite see where your path leads. That's okay. Give it time—but keep checking in with yourself.

There are countless examples of people starting something incredible in the second half of their lives. I had my last baby at 39 and opened a branch of a staffing company. When it's meant to be, it will find you. And your dreams only need to be as big as you want them to be.

Maybe your dream is as simple as planting a garden in your backyard, paying off a loan, buying a small piece of land, or finishing a book series. Your dreams don't have to be earth-shattering to be deeply fulfilling. Only you get to decide what matters.

And remember—it's okay to fail. In fact, you will fail. Probably more than once. Heck, you might even succeed for a while and then fail. That's all part of the process. Living your best life means showing up every day, giving it your all, and repeating the cycle—until it's time to pivot. Practice failing so you can learn.

It took experiencing the highs and lows of business to understand that we are meant to fail, then rise, then fail again—only to rise even higher. The expansions, the setbacks, the moments that felt like total collapse, only to rebuild again—that was me surviving, adapting, evolving. Figuring it out as I went.

Pursuing something big comes with imposter syndrome, self-doubt, self-judgment, and guilt—alongside celebration, courage, pride, and excitement. And always, a lingering sense of fear. Fear of what's next. Fear of falling. Fear of failing. But with every step higher, the view becomes a little more breathtaking—and a little more unsettling.

Achieving something you worked so hard for—finally reaching that milestone, celebrating for a moment—only to be met with grief, doubt, and the fear of losing it all. With every step forward comes the shedding of the old, and with it, the pain of letting go. Mourning one achievement, knowing there's still another climb ahead. No matter how many steps you take, there's always another—until you decide to stop.

Persistence is the foundation of any business. A little grit, a little determination, a lot of humility, and just a touch of crazy. It's about falling and getting back up, again and again. Sometimes, while others question your choices. Do it anyway. Do it for you.

We have the power to survive anything. If you're struggling right now, trust me on this—just take the next step. One foot in front of the other. Hold on to your faith, your belief in yourself, and do the next logical thing that feels right, weighing all possible outcomes. You are meant to get to the other side of this. A better side exists—you just need to find your way there.

You can do anything. You just need to know who you are, what you want, and take micro-movements toward it every single day. Time and money? They're excuses. If you want something badly enough, you will find a way. You'll find the grit. You'll survive the ebbs and flows. Time is yours to use, and money is rarely the real obstacle. If you're doing what you love, living in your vibration, opportunities will come. What's meant for you will find you—if you're open to receiving it, willing to work for it, and ready to chase it with everything you've got.

GO SMALL SO YOU CAN GO BIG

When I was younger, I knew a couple in my neighborhood with a wild goal: pay off their mortgage in just five years. Five years! They worked tirelessly, spent minimally, and made every decision with that goal in mind. And they did it.

Then? They traveled. A lot.

I still marvel at the sheer drive, discipline, and sacrifice that went into their decision. They were in their late twenties, maybe early thirties. And this wasn't some tiny house—it was at least 2,500 square feet in a beautiful neighborhood, just a few blocks from the ocean. I know, right?! He had a decent job; she was a stay-at-home mom who bought bad debt and made collection calls from home. They drank only water, ate every meal at home, and never splurged—not even on birthdays or anniversaries. But when those five years were up, they lived better than anyone.

Can you imagine the patience that took? I see it as practice. Because practice doesn't just build patience—it builds possibility.

My neighbor's 19-year-old daughter decided to become a bodybuilder. For almost a year, she trained relentlessly, weighed every bite of food, and skipped out on everything her peers were doing. Her commitment to her vibration—her purpose—was unshakable. The patience and discipline she endured to see her transformation unfold was unimaginable.

And she did it. She competed. She stepped away. And now? She's preparing to dive back in.

If you've ever known a bodybuilder, you know the process of coming out of training can be just as hard as going in. But that's the truth about any goal worth chasing. It's all hard. The question is—are you willing to do it anyway?

It's physically draining. It's mentally exhausting. Most people can't control their eating long enough to reach their goals—I can't even stick to a diet for three days!

My neighbor's daughter told me something at the end of her first bodybuilding training, right when she was shedding the last bit of fat—the hardest part. The part where you're weak, shaking, and starving. The part where you don't think you can do it anymore, but you're so close to the end goal that you have to find the discipline to push through. That's when she said:

"Now that I have done this, I know that for the rest of my life, I can do anything I set my mind to."

Wow. Imagine having that kind of realization at the very beginning of adulthood. It took me decades to even come close to understanding that. She found the passion, dedication, and commitment to do something most people wouldn't even dare to try.

We own a staffing company, and once, we had a gentleman working for us who had a pretty big secret. At the time, we had no idea, but he was homeless. Truly homeless.

This wasn't someone down on their luck without options—he was working a professional job at a well-known corporate facility. He had a cell phone, a car, and a gym membership. Every night, he slept in his car. Every morning, he went to the gym, worked out, showered, got dressed, and arrived at work on time—looking completely put together. He washed his clothes at a local laundromat. He ate meals at a shelter. And he never made excuses.

This man was willing to do whatever it took to better his life. He refused to let obstacles or setbacks stop him.

I have never been more impressed by anyone in my life.

Talk about persistence. Talk about grit. Talk about seeing a way through.

If you want something badly enough, you can achieve it. There are more than eight working hours in a day. You can have your day job, then come home and dedicate two hours to writing your screenplay—or whatever speaks to you. The key is communicating your goals, timelines, and the sacrifices you're willing to make to your loved ones.

I'm hopeful they'll support you. But if not, it might not be the right timing. In that case, make small adjustments every day to stay on course with the life you're meant to live.

If money is the obstacle, start saving. Even if it's just five dollars a week—start. Until you begin, nothing will change. You either take baby steps toward your happiness, or you stay stuck. Time will pass either way.

Let's face it—money is important. And when there's not enough, it can lead to stress. But too many people believe that money only comes from one place: their nine-to-five job. That's simply not true.

Growing up, my dad always said, "If you need money, just go get it." Seemed simple enough. Yes, that nine-to-five job might be your primary source of income, but if it's not enough to meet your needs or wants, go get more. Get a second job or start a side hustle. Now, there are so many flexible opportunities: delivery services, driving gigs, weekend jobs, and more. These options not only keep you from spending, but spending less also means saving more.

It all adds up—and it gives you purpose and hope. But you can't sit back and wait for everything to magically fall into place. If you need money, go get it.

The mindset that life doesn't just happen to you is empowering. You are walking through life, interacting with everything that comes your way. You choose your path, and you choose to change it. You choose your people. You choose how something or someone makes you feel. You choose how your day begins and ends.

Your choices determine what happens next. You are 100% in control of you, your emotions, and your outcome. Read that again.

ONLY YOU DETERMINE YOUR VALUE

We live in the Tampa Bay area, where baseball legend Derek Jeter played spring training for the New York Yankees. Derek built a 22,000 square foot mansion, making it the largest home in Tampa Bay. Custom-built on the water, it became a major topic of conversation in the community. Many of us watched as the construction progressed. If you were lucky enough to pass by boat, you could witness the transformation firsthand—from the lot being cleared, to the infrastructure going up, to the massive pool taking shape. We were all captivated by the idea of such a dream coming to life in our own hometown. Derek Jeter and his family moved in after the home was completed in 2011, but not long after, they relocated to Miami.

And guess what happened next? Our beloved Tampa Bay Buccaneers made a huge splash by signing none other than Tom Brady as their quarterback. Not only did the city have Super Bowl dreams, but we also hoped for a glimpse of Tom Brady or his stunning wife, Giselle. When Tom rented Derek's house, we were star-struck. That is, until a massive fence went up. Understandable, right? With boaters and onlookers with cameras and binoculars, privacy became a must. But, just like Derek and his family, Tom and Giselle decided that the mansion wasn't quite the right fit for them either.

So, what happened next? A developer swooped in and purchased the sprawling mansion for $22.5 million—about $1,000 per square foot—making it the highest-priced home sale in Tampa Bay history. We were initially disappointed not to see another celebrity in residence. But then came the real shock: the mansion, just a few years old, was slated to be demolished. Rumor had it that three smaller properties were planned for the site. Can you believe it? A recently built dream home—gone.

It turns out, even the most impressive homes sometimes aren't good enough. And that's a lesson we all can learn from.

So, what's the point of all of this? Just like the dirt at 58 Bahama Circle, people will always have opinions about our life and our value. To some, we'll be as desirable as that mansion—a place to call home. To others, we may seem like something that needs to be torn down and rebuilt. Some may never think we're good enough, constantly needing more. Our perceived value often shifts based on the observer at that moment. But the truth is, our real value lies within. You get to decide your value, and you don't need to sell out to anyone.

You control what your worth is. You choose what you will accept, and you choose what you'll deny. The things around us may change, the people in our lives may change, but the core of who we are remains the same. We evolve, but our true vibration is always with us. Our value should be determined by no one but ourselves.

The good news? We decide who we let in and whose opinions we'll accept. Our authentic value is ours to define, but sometimes, we let others cloud our judgment. We internalize their doubts. The judgments of others can alter our perception, but we don't have to let them, and we absolutely should not. Make sure the people you allow into your headspace not only see your value but want to add to it.

If we check in with ourselves every day, seeking self-improvement—not just to better our lives but to refine our perspective—then we'll hardly have time for others' opinions. Sometimes, we need to look inward and adjust how we interact with others. Other times, we need to focus on the horizon to ensure we're on the best path, seeing life from the best vantage point.

Outsiders who are looking in have no idea what we're truly capable of. All they see are the obstacles in our way. They don't see our thoughts, our determination, or the heart behind our actions. Your dreams, your goals, and your actions are yours to manage. You are the CEO, COO, and CFO of YOU, Inc. Others will doubt you because they are not you.

Real time life: I love that my 13-year-old daughter just showed me an Instagram post she'd made, asking if I'd seen it. I replied, "I think so. Did I like it?" Her response? "I don't know, I don't look at my likes!"

Dear Lord, can we all do that, please?! Those likes do not define our worth. Your posts are your expressions, your moments in time, your memories. I like to think of it as my online scrapbook. Those likes and comments say nothing about who you are or what you offer. Don't even look at them. And definitely don't let them affect your emotions, your thoughts, or your self-worth.

I know I may have lost some of you at, "My 13-year-old has an Instagram account." If that's you, you might have missed the point. But don't miss my suggestion to skip the social media likes and comments. Your value isn't measured by them.

SPEAKING OF SOCIAL MEDIA

Be mindful of how you treat others and how you engage on social media. The old saying still holds true: if you don't have anything nice to say, don't say anything at all. Stay out of online conflicts. Avoid posting things that you wouldn't say in person. Don't share comments that might make someone feel bad—it's simply unnecessary.

In the short term, venting online might feel good, but the relief won't last. The damage caused by such comments often lingers far longer. This kind of behavior doesn't create positive change—it breeds negativity. And sometimes, that negativity can consume you.

The same applies to real life. Stay true to your vibration, but remember—you don't have to be mean to others. If making small adjustments to accommodate someone else's feelings leads to the same outcome, then do it. If you can avoid commenting when there's no need for it, then do that too. Sometimes, the best response is to say nothing at all.

Bottom line: be kind. Because practice makes positive.

FORECASTING

Visualizing your future looks from every perspective: seeing it from your current point of view, your future self, and even the perspective of your loved ones. The changes you make today may or may not lead you to where you want to be down the road.

I ran into an old acquaintance during a walk one day—someone I used to take yoga classes with. During that time, she became certified to teach and eventually became one of the instructors at our yoga studio. We had brief conversations before and after class about life, but nothing too deep. For those of you familiar with yoga, you know that it often releases emotions and creates a unique connection between people, simply from practicing together. Yoga is, after all, a community.

When we bumped into each other years later, she told me something that completely floored me: "You saved my marriage." I was completely flabbergasted. I asked her to elaborate, and when she did I was overwhelmed with joy and peace. She explained that I had opened her eyes to a perspective on divorce she hadn't considered before. Sometimes, we're so caught up in the present moment—the kids, jobs, daily obligations—that we forget to look beyond the immediate struggles. Life can feel like a never-ending to-do list: volleyball practice, soccer games, dinner... we're just trying to survive the schedule.

In the midst of that chaos, a marriage can suffer. It's easy to fall into the trap of thinking, I'm not happy, and it must be my spouse's fault. We often forget that the children, who are our hearts, aren't the cause of our unhappiness—so it must be our spouse. We convince ourselves that if we leave, happiness will follow. But more often than not, that's not the answer. While divorce might be the solution in some cases, it's important to pause and reflect deeply. When the to-do list becomes overwhelming, we tend to get trapped in the "I do more" or "it's not fair" game. And that game, unfortunately, always ends ugly.

Co-parenting with an ex-partner—and their families—can present a whole new set of challenges. It's not just your ex; it's their parents, their siblings, too. After a divorce, you may find yourself left with a sense of loneliness, mourning the loss of the family unit and the fairytale of happily ever after. The hardest part of divorce is that you still have to parent together, and you remain the nuclear family to your children. Forever, she will be mom, and he will be dad. That never stops.

So now, the person is still in your life, but you no longer have each other's interests as a main concern. This could even lead to more fighting or more family turmoil. Ask yourself: is it my spouse that I'm mad at, or is it the way they're reacting to our current season of life?

I promise, if you haven't felt it yet, there will come a time in your life when your spouse disappoints you, lets you down, or simply makes you mad as heck. Just as your parents have, or your children, or your siblings, or your best friend, you'll experience moments of discomfort in every relationship. You'll have your ins and outs, ups and downs, throughout your entire life. There's no getting around that.

I would guess that interactions with ex-spouses are rarely pleasurable. It might even become more challenging when your ex has a new spouse or more children, and then—if that new spouse has children from a previous marriage—your children now have half-siblings and step-siblings, with relationships that will extend outside of you. I'm not saying it won't be blissful, but I am saying there will be new layers to consider—things that, as the ex-spouse, you get zero say in, because it's no longer your space of responsibility.

There are two things in life that seriously change you: love and grief. These two things will make your vibration skip a beat. Be cautious with them.

The one and only thing you can control in every interaction with anyone, at any time, is the way you respond to them, to the situation, and to your feelings. That's it. You are in control of your response. You might want to contemplate that fact deeply because it can determine the course of your life.

Sometimes we get so mad at someone that we sever the relationship due to the pain and hurt. And sometimes, we absolutely need to sever the tie. The relationship may be toxic for us, and our lives may be better for it. But sometimes, that decision leaves a hole we carry around forever, leaving us wondering, Was it worth it? Could I have responded differently, and things wouldn't have ended so poorly?

Whether it was a family member, a friend, or a spouse, if the connection was deep enough, when it comes to an end, it can leave a scar. It can change who we are from that day forward. It can also change the way we interact with other important relationships in our lives. It can change who we allow into our lives.

PRACTICE makes POSITIVE

This point stuck with my yoga friend. I encouraged her to imagine ten years after a divorce: to see her husband married to someone else, to see that person interacting with her children. I asked her to picture a whole other world her children would be a part of, and that she wouldn't. Once she saw that side of her decision, she decided to stay in the marriage and try to make it work. She didn't want to lose that much control over her family. She wanted to remain the woman in her family. And it worked. Years later, they are still together and seem very happy. For that, I am grateful.

This is why we must think through all our decisions from every perspective. Imagine where you might be a year from now, ten years from now, even decades from now, and what that might look like.

BIG DECISIONS SHOULD NEVER BE MADE LIGHTLY.

Discovering What Completes Us

DISCOVERING PURPOSE

When you're not doing the things that fuel your soul and aren't living in alignment with your vibration, things just don't feel right. You might even become ill. We all have an innate need to feel valued and to have purpose in our community. If we spend time doing things that seem to lack meaning, we become disengaged. It's important to understand that the work we put in has a purpose, and it goes somewhere.

Research has shown that we all tend to learn in different ways. Some of us learn through hearing, some by seeing, others through physical actions or kinesthetically, and some through reading and writing. Wouldn't it make sense, then, that we experience life differently and need different experiences to fulfill us? Isn't that what the newer workforce is requiring? Millennials, for example, value experiences, personalization, authenticity, and transparency. Many want to know why they're doing the work they're doing and how it contributes to the greater good.

A friend I'll call Sally had an amazing corporate job working for a huge company. It came with a big salary and all the dreamy perks. Her profession came easily to her—she was good at what she did. But her vibration was off. Sally became so miserable with her day-to-day obligations that it was starting to affect her physically. She felt lethargic, had stomach pains, and even developed shingles. She had lost belief in the value of what she was doing, and this disconnect with her internal vibration was manifesting in physical consequences.

Sally made minor changes each day to get back to her happiness. One of the first things she did was look for alternative ways to create income streams so she wouldn't be so reliant on her paycheck. She also made sure to take her vacation days, log off at a certain time, and not let work consume her. Eventually, she left her corporate job and started her own company where her passion could thrive. Sally continues to make small adjustments to get her vibration back in order, but now she's chasing happiness and purpose, not the corporate ladder.

The feeling of purpose is important for more than just our happiness; it's crucial for our health as well. A sense of purpose in life is strongly linked to both physical and mental well-being. Studies have even shown that those with a sense of purpose tend to live longer, sleep better, and have a more robust immune system. They experience lower stress levels and enjoy better brain function.

When we're doing what we love and feeling valued in our contributions, we're in full vibration. And life is simply better with that little beat.

CHECKING IN DAILY FOR THE MAGIC

One thing I've learned to love about my husband is that he worries about things, so I don't have to. I did have to learn to love this because he's a "glass is half empty" kind of person. In fact, his picture could probably be in the dictionary next to the definition. I, on the other hand, am more of an "everything happens for a reason; my glass is always overflowing" kind of person. In most relationships, there's a dreamer and a realist. I am certainly the dreamer, and I'm so grateful for his structure and foundation as the realist in my life. I'm thankful he believes in my dreams and does everything he can to help make them come true.

My daughter recently found out I was working on this book, and her response was, "You always have some new idea or dream you're working on." She told me she thinks I have a problem. She wasn't exactly saying this in the kindest way. But I get it—I do start a lot of things, and most of them don't go anywhere. But when they do, it's magical.

The whole point of life, and of learning about yourself, is checking in with yourself daily. Living in your vibration means trying new things out, even if they don't fit or go anywhere. If you don't try something, you'll never know if it feels right. How else do you learn? If you don't try new things, how do you evolve? We try on outfits before we buy them, so why not try on different ideas? One thing that allows me this luxury is my husband. His rules, processes, and budgets keep us grounded and, in a roundabout way, fuel my dreams. Be sure to recognize and appreciate the differences in your partnerships.

I once heard that there is a female and a male answer to every possible decision. Even if you don't have a partner, you should look to both sides within yourself before you move too quickly. We all have a feminine side and a male side within us. Consult both frequently. Don't stay on one side too long, or the other side may become paralyzed. This can throw you off balance. You need to be balanced within before you can balance in a marriage.

Check in with your spouse often. This is your person, your other half. It's the life you share together that should be the mutual connection, the foundation on which to stand together and strategize life goals.

I once heard that your spouse could fill 90 to 95 percent of your love cup, but 100% is perfection, and no one is perfect. Sometimes, after years of marriage, that missing 5 to 10 percent starts to scream. Sometimes, all you see is the 5 to 10 percent they aren't doing or can't be. If only they were more whimsical, more clean, more adventurous, more responsible—whatever it is that's missing—you must remind yourself it's only 5 or 10 percent. Someone might come along and seem to satisfy that missing percentage, but they might only sizzle for 5 to 10 percent of the time. Like a match, they burn bright but not for long, and then you'll miss the 90 to 95 percent you once had.

When I was that little girl in second grade, my dream job was to be a stay-at-home mom. Yep, that was my answer. Dream big, little girl! On top of that, I wanted to be a wife who met my husband at the door with a kiss after a long day's work. I think I watched too much Bewitched when I was young. After women fought for decades for independence and equality, I wanted to serve my family.

Well, I held onto that dream for a lot of my life. I didn't want to just sit back and be pampered. I wanted to be there for every moment of my children's lives. I didn't want to miss a thing. I also wanted to support my husband and his dreams. There was something about being the woman beneath his wings that excited me. I was able to achieve this dream while most of my children were young.

Of course, we weren't rich by any means, but I was good at making a dollar stretch, and I was great at finding jobs I could do with my kids. I delivered newspapers, collected rent checks for a property management company, worked at their preschool, and babysat other children. I always found a way to make it work. I built my life around them, and I wouldn't change a thing.

When children reach a certain age, they start to grow their own roots. They begin to strategize their own paths, and naturally, they want to improve on the life they knew in their original family. Because I had built my life around them, it was now time for me to reinvent myself and detach a little. Someone once told me to simply care less. Not careless, like I could care less about you, but care—just care a little less. This is their life. They need to carve their own paths and probably need to make a few mistakes along the way. I'm still working on this chapter of my life, but the new grandbaby is making it a little easier. He gives the best baby snuggles.

There are so many things to look forward to in this new chapter. First and foremost—freedom! I've been a mother since I was 24 years old. Heck, I still have a 13-year-old at home. To say my life has been centered around children's busy schedules is an understatement. But now, I can sleep in some mornings, travel a little more, and explore that creative side within me. Not only is this book flowing out of me, but I have a screenplay and a country song knocking at my brain, begging me to give them life. I don't even know where this is coming from. The actor John Cena lives in our area, and goodness knows, the next time I see him at the grocery store, I plan to pitch him a movie idea! I'm not even sure I recognize myself.

I tell you all of this because we were never meant to only do one thing. We are complex vessels of life, thoughts, hopes, and aspirations. Creativity was a word I would never have used to describe myself, but as my life changes, I evolve as well. Maybe it's because I have more time now? Maybe it's less stress? Maybe I'm just exploring different extensions of myself? Or maybe it was always there, but I didn't recognize it. Whatever the reason, it's a part of me that has risen to the forefront. I believe our strengths and desires change as our life experiences change. I was probably very creative when my children were younger, but I didn't see it as such. I was just entertaining them. Now that they don't need that kind of entertainment, the creative side within me is looking for new outlets.

There is so much you have to offer the world. You simply need to find your vibration every day, in every new circumstance. Be you. The ever-evolving, true version of you. Wait for the right time. Once it comes, and the timing is right, it will flow through you and out of you into the world. The more you feed it and give it life, the more you put your vibration first—above everything else—the more you will thrive.

FRIENDSHIPS COMPLETE US

Our neighborhood is a close-knit community. For the last seventeen years, we've raised children together, witnessed career changes, gone back to school, celebrated anniversaries, weddings, births, divorces, graduations, made good and bad decisions, had parties, holidays, sickness, and the loss of parents—tears and laughter, you name it. We've done it all, and through it all, we've supported each other. We are best friends. Our husbands are best friends, and some of our children are best friends too.

We know what we have is special, and we truly cherish it. I'm pretty sure that if we ever move, we'll all move together. At least, I'm hopeful. I'm not sure I could do life without them at this point. We joke about growing old together.

Some of us just got back from a weekend at a yoga camp, and we can't stop texting each other with encouraging words. We never tire of each other. Because of them, I have the support to write this book. We encourage each other to dream, channel our goals, and work toward improving ourselves. We are in a constant state of self-awareness and growth, helping each other move in the best direction possible. We listen to each other, motivate each other, celebrate each other, and we also mourn for each other.

Life is just a little easier when you're held accountable by people you love and trust. My friends are supporting me on this crazy journey. My dream is to finish this book, travel to promote it, and host workshops to inspire others to live within their vibration. You'll have to let me know if it works out for you.

My friend groups extend beyond my neighborhood. I have friends at the gym, friends I go on girls' trips with, friends from high school, friends from my hometown, and even Facebook friends. Friendships are so important. They're where we can be silly, test ideas, be vulnerable, and feel connected to our femininity.

PRACTICE *makes* POSITIVE

Please, if you give yourself nothing else in the world, give yourself friendship. Join a group—there are tons on Facebook. Take a class at the gym and talk to someone. Start a book club with your neighbors. Reach out to someone who comes to mind. They might be craving it as much as you are. Don't give up until you find the friends who vibe with you, and then nurture those friendships.

So many relationships stumble over the idea of fairness: "I do more, I try harder, I'm always the planner, I'm always the one who reaches out. It's not fair!" Who cares? If you feel good when you're together, then be the one to reach out! If you're getting what fills your soul and your cup, then keep doing more. This applies to home and work too. If you can do more, just do more. It usually pays off, but do it because you can. If someone steps in to help, be grateful, but also willing and happy to do all that you can.

There are many who would love to have what you consider a burden. Do everything you can, with the hope to say at the end of the day, "Today was a good day, and I did all that I could." I know from experience that knowing this builds a positive outlook.

We need many different people in our lives, in different circles. Each person will offer something unique, completing or bringing out a different version of you. You'll also find fulfillment in offering your personal strengths to different people. For instance, in your close-knit friendship group, you might not be the most outgoing one, but in your book club, you might be the most social. You might find that you can be a different version of yourself with each group. You could even encourage someone in one group to be more social or outgoing in a smaller setting.

We each shine brightest in different environments. What you learn from one group can be applied to another, making each group dynamic uniquely yours. You can't get everything you need from just one person, and you can't be everything to someone else. But you can experiment with different personality traits, trying them on with different people until they feel more natural. You have layers and depth, so embrace the evolving versions of yourself. Don't pretend to be someone you're not, but don't be afraid to sharpen a personality trait that might not come naturally right away. If you feel it inside, it's still a part of you—it might just be quieter for now.

Think of the rings on your Apple watch. Each group represents a different circle, and each circle is best filled by that specific group. Your friends at church support your spiritual side, while others might feed your intellectual, creative, or playful sides. You'll need different people at various moments—daily, monthly, and throughout the year. So, be sure to maintain friendships with as many different groups as you can, not just your favorite ones. Those special relationships are vital, but you still need others to thrive as well.

Blue might be your favorite color, but you don't want to wear only blue. Spaghetti might be your favorite meal, but you don't want it for breakfast, lunch, and dinner. The same goes for friendships. You need a variety of friends to meet the different needs and circles in your life. You'll thrive in different groups in unique ways, offering different strengths to each. Sometimes you'll be teaching or leading, and other times you'll be learning or following. Don't let yourself get pigeonholed into just a select few friendships—life has a way of surprising us.

One of the most significant mental health struggles in America is a lack of community. We all want to fit in, to be part of a group, to feel liked, connected, and valued. Without this connection, isolation can creep in, leading to depression, which can wreak havoc in many areas of your life. Finding community in as many ways and places as possible is essential for your well-being.

In high school, the kids who play sports, join clubs, and know everyone always seem the most popular and happy. It's because they are connected. They have teammates and a passion for their athletics. They belong to multiple circles of friends because they've joined clubs with different causes and common purposes. It's easy to get to know people when you have something in common. Common ground comes from a shared purpose.

This doesn't have to end when you become an adult. You can still find meaningful connections by joining groups and activities—whether it's the Rotary Club, volunteering at a local Boys & Girls Club, supporting the Red Cross, contributing at church, joining a Facebook group, or taking a class at a community college just for fun. There's always something to try.

A friend's daughter, in her late twenties, recently joined a knitting group where everyone else is at least twice her age. She loves it. Not only is she sharpening her knitting skills, but she's also teaching the group a few tricks of her own. She's part of other groups with people her age, but she's expanding her circle—diversifying in both interests and age. This is exactly what everyone should do.

You don't need to be best friends with everyone, but being part of a variety of groups with different people, ages, and backgrounds is important. From each group, you take something, and you give something in return. You need exposure to different perspectives and knowledge bases. Take what you like and leave what doesn't resonate with you. Likewise, others will appreciate what you bring to the table. We give and take, learn and teach, all through community and variety.

As we move through different phases of life, our interests change, and we need different things from different people at various times. Staying fluid and adaptable to these shifts is key.

Lastly, build connections and communities by showing up for others. Make an effort to be there for graduations, birthdays, retirement parties, and holidays. Celebrate the milestones and monumental moments in others' lives. Be present for the good times, and share in the joy of your community.

GETTING WHAT YOU WANT

It's so easy to focus on what isn't coming our way. Why does what we want seem so hard to achieve? Even though we're doing everything we can to get there, it always feels just out of reach. It's easy to fall into the trap of self-pity and discouragement.

Sometimes, you want something so badly that you spend years chasing it. You study, lay the groundwork, prepare, and take huge leaps to reach your goal. Then, one day, someone you know—maybe a coworker or a friend—gets the exact thing you've been working so hard to achieve. They didn't prepare, they didn't put in half the time and energy you have, and yet, it just seems to fall in their lap. You might wonder, Why not me? Maybe even get angry about it.

But the truth is, we don't know what others have been through or what's been happening behind the scenes. Perhaps life has been quietly preparing them for this moment since childhood. Maybe they've been experiencing a series of micromovements in their life, ones you couldn't even see. What you've consciously focused on for a few years, they might have been focused on for their entire lives—just on a subconscious level. And then one day, a door closes in their life, and a window opens. Suddenly, that thing you've been working toward for years just falls into their lap.

So much of what we experience in life seems to follow a similar pattern. We learn to walk around the same age. We start school around the same age. We may get married, have children, and experience life's milestones at similar times. It often feels like we're walking parallel paths with our friends, peers, and coworkers.

Yet, each person experiences a different childhood, a different socio-economic background, family dynamics, and unique interactions with the world based on the opportunities they're presented with and the timing of when they're exposed to them. We go through different shifts, big and small, that shape who we are and how we think. Some of us leap toward an opportunity, while others take their time to strategize. Neither approach is right or wrong—until we make a decision. Hindsight is 20/20, but our individual thoughts and strategies are meant to be unique, with unique outcomes.

Take Tiger Woods. He became an expert in his sport—was it natural talent? Was it the result of years of practice? Was it because his father exposed him to golf at such an early age? Yes, to all of the above. His path was shaped from the time he was in a high chair. Anyone entering the golf world at the same time, no matter how skilled, couldn't compete with him. No matter how much they practiced, they could never change their first exposure to the sport or match his natural ability.

But what we often don't see are the parts of his childhood that went into that reward. I don't know much about Tiger's personal feelings or childhood, but let's imagine, hypothetically, that he didn't like golf. Maybe he wanted to play soccer with the neighborhood kids while his dad made him practice golf instead. If someone you see seems to have things come easy to them, it might have come at an expense. Maybe they paid their dues earlier in life in ways you can't see—working harder, hustling more, taking bigger chances.

All I can say is this: chase your own happiness and don't compare yourself to others. Comparison only brings sadness. Sometimes it's your turn, and sometimes it's not. Life is about trying, positioning yourself in the right spot, and hoping that this is the wave you get to ride. But keep going. Success comes to us when the time is right for each of us.

FAMILY TIES

The nuclear family comes in many shapes and sizes. I define it as the one you grew up with and the one you create with your spouse or significant other. Both are important, and both provide experiences that shape who you are and influence what you'll become or achieve in life. You might feel closer to different people in your family at different times. Maybe you're closer to one sibling because you live near each other. Maybe you're closer to another because your kids are the same age. Maybe you rely on one parent when buying a house and the other when you want to go to brunch. The best part about family is that the connection never truly goes away. It's a bond that lasts forever. You might get angry and not speak to a family member for years, but then something will happen that brings you back together. Even if you never speak again, there's still a connection. You might find yourself at their bedside should they fall ill or attending their funeral when their time comes. That is family.

The sharing of genetics can be a powerful force, even for siblings who have never met. If you find out about a half-sibling through an ancestry app, you might feel drawn to meet them—curious to see if they look, act, or think like you. An adopted child might seek out their biological parents, or vice versa. A child raised by an addicted parent might still feel the need to try and help that parent, no matter the cost.

A mother may love her child unconditionally, regardless of what that child does. We see this in murder trials, and as uncomfortable as it is, we all understand it. A mother's love is unwavering. Even in our court system, a wife doesn't have to testify against her husband, and vice versa. The family bond is something we've written into our justice system. Family is our first circle of trust—the people we can count on when all else fails. At least, we hope that's true for everyone. I understand that some don't have that, and I'm truly sorry for that.

If your original nuclear family isn't your ideal, you can create one of your own. You can make it big or small, setting your own traditions, teachings, and moral guidelines. You can have the family you've always desired. Remember, it's normal to want better than you had, and it's okay to adjust course when needed. Your role within both families will change and evolve throughout your life. Some phases you'll thrive in, and some you won't.

One of my favorite lessons my husband taught me was about my role as a mother. Keep in mind, I view my role as a mother as the most important one in my life. It's all I ever wanted to be, and I take immense pride in my children and my responsibilities to them.

This was easy for me when they were growing up. If they needed me, I was there. Need a ride? I'll take you. Hungry? Let me make something. Need your shoe tied or help with homework? I'm your girl. I was the doctor, the chef, the chauffeur, the party planner, the form filler, the cuddler, the braider, the shopper, the referee, the playmate, the audience, the orchestra, the director—the lead parent. You name it, I wanted to provide it. I liked to think of myself as their Mary Poppins.

Then something interesting happened that I wasn't exactly prepared for. Something that was meant to happen. In fact, it happened because my children had become well-adjusted and capable adults. They stopped needing me as much. They started doing more things on their own. They stopped consulting me. They stopped coming to the Mom Show every day. That's when my husband said the most profound words that helped me understand, accept the changes that were happening, and become excited about the future and the relationships I hold so dear.

He told me that for my whole adult life, I had been the director and the lead actress in my own life. The whole performance was dictated and directed by me, for me, and through me. But now, it was time for me to move into the supporting actress role. My children were starting their own productions, and I would be there to support them from the sidelines.

Wow. Profound. Not only did I feel a wave of relief wash over me, but I also began to see everything from a whole new perspective. I was happy to step aside and let go of the pressure of the hustle and bustle and all the responsibilities that had once been mine. Especially because now, I had VIP seating, backstage access, and the best supporting actress role in the world! Not to mention, the best partner to ride off into the sunset with. The transition might have been hard, but I really like this new space... a lot.

CONNECTIONS

I don't know if it's because of social media or the global pandemic, but it seems like people don't connect—or even interact—as much as they used to. I make it a point to say goodbye to my classmates at the gym on my way out, thank the instructor, and wave and smile at the people at the check-in desk. It seems to make people smile, and they seem to respond positively, but I'm not sure they would start the interaction if I didn't. I don't even know if they genuinely like it, or if it makes them uncomfortable on some level.

The world has come to a point where people are uncomfortable when someone says hello, and that really saddens me. I just worry that we're becoming more individualized than community-based. Maybe that's why so many are struggling with depression, social anxiety, and loneliness. I believe that's also why TikTok, in particular, has become so popular. It's an artificial form of communication. The person looks into the camera and enthusiastically shares a story, a song, a product they love, or even a joke with anyone who will watch. It feels like they're talking, singing, or smiling at and with someone. There's a connection—but it's shallow at best.

They wink, smile, and make eye contact. The audience reacts from the solitude of their own private space, but in their mind, they're connecting with this person. The brain sees it as reality because it looks and feels like reality. But it doesn't go anywhere because it can't. The person on the other end of the camera doesn't know you—they're not really with you. Put these same two people in a room together, and they probably wouldn't even make eye contact. But through the video, they feel connected.

The huge problem is that it's a one-way connection. The influencer doesn't know the person watching. The viewer isn't interacting with the influencer. They're only taking in what's presented. This isn't a true connection. During Covid, TikTok became very popular. We needed the artificial connection and interactions because we couldn't get them in the real world, but I'm afraid we got stuck in the artificial world and now don't know how to get out.

I feel that most of us are missing that human interaction and connection but have lost the ability to create or find it. We rely on one-way, artificial stimuli to fulfill our basic human need for social contact. The more time we spend in this artificial world, the more we lose the ability to connect with real people in the real world.

Please limit your screen time. Give some of your time to working toward making real-life connections. Look for groups that share your interests and take small steps to join. Start by making eye contact with someone. Once that feels normal, smile. Finally, say hello. Just see where it takes you. It might take a little practice, but it's still within you. Micro movements, setting goals, and daily check-ins will get you there. You need it. We all do. It's the best way to practice positivity.

The reason certain people become influencers is that they have a talent for connecting. But they also practice and edit—they cut and restart. They spend hours behind the scenes, especially when they're first starting, perfecting their skills.

You can practice, too. Stand in front of the mirror. Practice what you plan to say. Practice what you'll wear. Practice the gestures you'll use while talking. Practice what you think might be an appropriate response. Start with people you're already comfortable with. You'll become more confident, and then try your new skills on someone you might never see again. You have nothing to lose and everything to gain.

In my home, we practice speeches for school, interviewing skills, and difficult conversations we need to have with others. It's good to practice, but the interaction doesn't need to be perfect. Life isn't perfect, and people aren't perfect. In fact, imperfections are often what connect us the most. The bottom line is we're all the same on a primal level. We all want to feel productive, appreciated, loved, valued, and safe. We find this in community. Community is where we can learn and where we can teach. We can lean in and support each other.

Don't be too picky or selective when it comes to friendships and community. I'm not asking you to marry or move in with anyone. You absolutely need to be selective when it comes to a life partner. But a circle of friends you meet once a month doesn't need to be your end-all, be-all. You might join a pickleball group that's older, retired, and a little more competitive than you'd like, but you're still forming a community. Friendships can grow over time, and diverse groups can fill unique needs. Embrace them all. As you create many outlets and circles, the less desirable ones can naturally fall away. Wouldn't that be a fun problem to have?

If you're feeling lost or out of place in the world, do a 30-day reset. Choose no TV for a month. No alcohol for a month. Maybe give yourself one day a week off from the restriction if that's what you need for overall success. But take the time to find out who you are, what you want, and where you're going. Make a shift in habit and routine to see things from a new perspective.

You need to stop the noise to really hear yourself and know what you want. Sit outside whenever you can. Without your phone. That one's tough for many of us. It'll be challenging at first; your mind will automatically search for it. You might only make it a minute or two the first time, but keep going. Keep trying. Do it every day for a month and see if you can go longer and longer. I promise that by the end of 30 days, your time in quiet, in comfort with that quiet, and without distractions, will bring you peace and clarity. Call it a cleanse for your soul. Challenge yourself to see if, for even one minute, you can find yourself with nothing but your thoughts. Reset your mind, your thoughts, and your actions. The outcomes will be automatic, wonderful—and positive.

SEASONS

One of the beautiful parts of life is its seasons. These seasons don't follow a calendar, nor can you predict them. They don't last for a set time, nor do they follow a specific order. There's no way to know what's coming next or when your current season will end.

As we move through life's seasons, we come to understand ourselves—our strengths, our weaknesses, and how we respond to challenges. It's hard to know how you'll react to a situation until you're in it. You might even surprise yourself. Looking back on past seasons can bring humility as you enter a new one. Some reflections may give you newfound confidence, having endured something difficult. The more seasons you experience, the better you know yourself—the strengths you lean on, the weaknesses you navigate, and the compassion that flows through you.

Sometimes, we find ourselves in winter—when life feels cold and barren. There's little to harvest, and we hunker down, waiting for better days. A winter season can come from the loss of a job, a loved one, or even the loss of motivation. During these times, we must turn inward and be still. Be patient. Be kind. Be quiet. This is a time for less. Spend less. Do less. Fight less. Just be. Let yourself rest, read, and reflect.

Winter can be sad, even scary—a season where you wonder if you can keep going. But I like to remind myself that things can only get better from here. A new season is always around the corner, and winter teaches us to appreciate the brighter days ahead. This doesn't mean stopping life or shutting yourself away—it simply means moving a little softer and slower than usual.

Spring is a time of new growth. You might feel more alive during the spring seasons of your life. Maybe you've started a new job, planned a vacation, or decided to take a new direction and try something different. Perhaps you've met a new love interest. Whatever it is, you are excited and energized. This is when you should take chances. Walk a path you haven't been on before. Explore yourself and the world around you. During this season, everything seems to go right—you can almost do no wrong. You feel lucky. You feel loved. You feel appreciated. You feel ambitious. It's important to enjoy this time. Stop and smell the roses. Lay in a hammock. Be one with nature. Do something amazing.

Summer is a season for hard work. Opportunities are there, and you need to capitalize on them so they can grow properly and produce. This is the time to work late, spend extra time with a friend or loved one in need, deep clean the house, or purge your closet. Work hard now so you can play hard later. This is a time of focus and determination. Get serious about your goals. Start a new workout. Take on a new project. Do all you can—physically and mentally—to get ahead.

Autumn is a season of harvest. It's the time to celebrate, feast, and enjoy the fruits of your labor. Maybe a child is getting married, you earned a promotion, or you finally completed a long-term project. Breathe it in and hold it close to your mind and heart. The harvest is what carries you through the harder seasons. It's a time of celebration when hard work has paid off, and you can finally enjoy the rewards. You feel full. Satisfied. Content. Warm. Nostalgic. You know you've done a good job, and the world feels right.

No one knows what season you're in except you—and maybe you're not even sure. Seasons aren't always extreme. Likewise, you don't know what season others are in either. This is why kindness is so important. You might be thriving in spring while someone else is struggling through winter. As you can imagine, these interactions require self-awareness and compassion.

Interestingly, you can experience all four seasons in a single day. Those are the days when you question everything. You might find yourself wondering, Did I even eat today? Or you might walk through the door and sigh, Oh, what a day today was!

Most seasons, however, last a while. They come and go with no particular order, timing, or reason. And that, my friends, is what I like to call life.

Much like the seasons of life, friendships also have their own cycles. People may enter your life for a reason, a season, or a lifetime—and they may leave for the same reasons. A reason could be a move, a breakup, or a chance meeting. A season might be school, a job, or simply a brief but meaningful time together. And, of course, a lifetime means forever—perhaps a family member, a spouse, or a best friend.

Just remember, what is meant to be will be, and what is meant for you will find its way. Enjoy the people in your life while they're here. Treat them well. Remember them fondly. Welcome them back if they return—so long as they're good for your energy. You can't force things, and sometimes, the harder you try, the clearer it becomes that it's just not right. Appreciate what was, and trust that something new will take its place. It might not be better or worse—just different.

Transitions are the hard part—the muddy part. Moving from one phase of life to another is strange, uncomfortable, scary, and unsettling. It's like shedding an exoskeleton. Growth and evolution are necessary, but they can be painful or, at the very least, uncomfortable. Even when a transition leads to something better, it can still feel nerve-racking and uncertain. We might wonder if we're ready, if we're good enough, or if we'll even like this new chapter.

Where we are now feels easy. We've mastered it. We can do it mindlessly, effortlessly. We know what to expect and how life feels here. We've excelled in this space. But that doesn't necessarily mean it's a healthy place. You could be in jail and about to be released to start fresh—clearly a move toward something better, yet you may have grown accustomed to the routine, no matter how bad it was. Maybe you're heading to rehab, but you became a pretty good addict. The truth is, if you've done something long enough—whether it's good for you or not—you've likely gotten pretty good at it. Whatever you're moving on from, the shift is happening because of growth on some level.

Sometimes, we've simply outgrown a space, or it's no longer working for us. Maybe that chapter naturally came to an end, or we made the decision to move on. Whatever the reason, transition is inevitable. It could be a job change, a birth, a death, a child going to college, a business closing or selling, a divorce, a marriage—anything that takes you from one reality to another. You will experience many of these in your life. Some will be welcome, and others will not. But one way or another, the transition will happen, and you will find yourself in a new situation. You will transition.

The way you respond to transitions is pivitol. Not only does it define who you are, but it also shapes who you become. Think of a caterpillar turning into a butterfly, a hermit crab moving into a new shell, or a crustacean shedding its exoskeleton. All of them are extremely vulnerable during transition—out of control and susceptible to danger. They must let go, trust the process, and hope for the best.

As a human, you experience all of that and more. During transitions, you must find grace, kindness, and humility. Leave the place you're transitioning from intact—without harm, without judgment, without regret. Preserve relationships whenever possible, and part ways with admiration. Be thankful for the time spent in that space—the lessons learned, the memories made, and the season you lived through.

That space was once a treasured or necessary part of your life and should be treated with respect. It brought you to where you are now. It was the path you chose—or needed—to take to become who you are today. It will always be a part of you. You will carry pieces of it into your next chapter and throughout your memories.

Transitions may require you to lean on others. Be grateful. Be vulnerable. Trust that you will make it through. Don't rush the process, but be mindful of the opportunities and paths ahead. Staying in transition too long can leave you feeling lost. Pay attention to yourself and those around you. Remember who stood by you during your transitions—those are your people. And when their time comes, be there for them too.

Pay attention to the pathways ahead of you. Consider where you want to go, who you want to be, what you want to carry with you, and what you want to leave behind. This is a time for spiritual growth—a time to discover who you are becoming. You should know more coming out of this phase than when you went in. Be sure to recognize the lessons. You will soon move into a new space where learning will begin again, but take the knowledge from your past with you as you move forward. Otherwise, that experience will have been for nothing.

Once you reach the next step—the new space—it will take time, but eventually, you'll feel comfortable again. You should be stronger, wiser, and more confident. The transition may have been uncomfortable, and you might never want to go through something like that again, but no matter where you end up on the other side, you will be okay.

You might not be as happy or as wealthy in this new space. Sometimes, a new space feels like a downgrade. Your life may feel less fulfilled. Perhaps you're retiring from a career you loved. Maybe you're becoming an empty nester. Or maybe you were in the NFL and got injured.

You may have lost everything you hold dear. Maybe you lost a spouse, a job, a home, or your health. Perhaps your transition was tragic. But in time, you will find a new normal. You will find peace in the newfound calm and stillness. Take the time to settle into the newness. Sometimes, we simply need to accept that the old space is over. It's no longer an option. It was with us, but now it is no more. We must find a new reason to be. Keep the memories, enjoy them from time to time, but don't live in the past. There is a new version of you—she has evolved, changed through experience, but she's still you.

Create new things. Find new happiness. Build new relationships. Form new patterns. Accept that this is where you are meant to be right now. Be the best version of yourself in this new circumstance. Find your new vibration.

Perhaps your new space is a great one! Perhaps you've just landed your dream job, met the love of your life, or reached a goal you set for yourself. Amazing! Good for you! Enjoy it wholeheartedly. You deserve this happiness. I want you to seal this moment and these feelings into your brain, your heart, your soul, and your vibration. These are the best days—the ones you want to remember. Appreciate them. Be thankful. Most of all, just enjoy them. Really enjoy them. Soak them up, then jump back in and soak up some more. I'm not kidding; you must embrace the good space and time while you're in it. Don't let it pass by without acknowledging it and fully experiencing it. Love every second.

During times of joy and happiness, remember to stay humble and kind. Keep in mind those who remain in the past—the people and memories you once shared space with. It's okay to leave them behind and move on. You've outgrown that space and time, and I'm not asking you to look back, but to move forward with honor, grace, and kindness.

Sometimes, paths go in circles, returning to where we once were, or they may cross again down the road. Make sure that if the past comes back to you, you can welcome it. Leave it better than you found it, and ensure you won't feel ashamed if you meet it again down the line.

There will be many transitions in your life. Learn to accept them, look forward to them, and see where they might take you. They will happen, so be open, receptive, and adaptable.

YOU ARE THE DRIVER

Most of us are in control of where we're going and where we've been. Sometimes, there are circumstances we're born into, or brought into through loved ones, that are beyond our control. Hopefully, we can find help to get out of or through such situations if they're bad or negative. But if we're in a situation of our own making, the choice is ours.

I've said it before, and I'll say it again: YOU are the only one in control of your happiness. If you're not happy or fulfilled, you're the only one who can make a change. You can blame it on your situation, but you're the one who got yourself there, and you're the only one who can get yourself out.

I absolutely hate the way my husband drives. He's constantly moving in and out of traffic, weaving back and forth between lanes, barely missing other cars. It feels like being in a bad video game, and I'm convinced it will ultimately be my cause of death. However, he sees everything. He can see fifteen cars ahead of him and anticipate their moves, reacting almost before they even happen. If only we could all translate this skill into our everyday life. If only we could predict the future before it happens and plan accordingly.

Imagine navigating your life like the lanes of traffic—driving through your life's decisions. Daily check-ins can help you get there. It takes planning and foresight. It takes responding with thought, but more than anything, it requires moments of quiet with yourself.

Ever notice how two siblings can experience the same upbringing but turn out completely different? Or how multiple people can experience the same trauma but react to it so differently? It's all about how each person reacts, interprets, and allows trauma to affect them. It's also about predicting what comes next—during the trauma or afterward. It seems the ones who can see past the trauma are the ones who adjust better. They can see a way through, a way out. Just like my husband with his driving. They respond to it almost simultaneously as it happens.

People who have this skill and those who do not differ in that one is in control of their response to the trauma, while the trauma controls the other. The ones in control have a sense of power and detachment, which keeps them feeling safe and agile. Unfortunately, the others are reliving the trauma on a loop. They let the trauma become a part of them and carry it everywhere. They become victims of the trauma, and their lives reflect this.

On a basic level, there seem to be two categories of people: victims and survivors. Victims are powerless and helpless in their situations. Survivors, on the other hand, are constantly looking for a way around or out. They are always assessing the situation and formulating a plan of attack or strategy.

There are people who interact with life and those who simply take what comes to them. It's important to take the good from every experience and leave the bad behind. Learn the lesson, move on, and try not to find yourself repeating the same lesson. Forgive those who hurt you. Understand that they might have had a lesson to learn through it all as well. Assume that's why you were brought together—to each learn your own lesson. Now that it's over, take the lesson and move on. Take the good from it and leave the rest by the side of the road in the past. It no longer serves you.

Most people just want to be heard. If you've ever been to therapy or taken a psychology class, you know that validating someone's feelings can be as simple as repeating what they've just said to you. You don't have to agree with it, but just validating that you've heard them can make all the difference.

When I was in college, working toward the degree I intended to use for Elementary Education, one of my instructors told a story that speaks to this. Does anyone remember the tape recorders where you could record your voice or music onto a cassette tape? Do we all know what a cassette tape is? Maybe we need a pause for a quick Google search here. You had to hit the record button, but there was also a pause button. You could press the pause button, and it would stop the recording. When you released the pause, it would continue. Easy, and easy to teach children to use.

This instructor shared that early in her teaching career, she spent too much of her day listening to children complain about each other. "Sally pulled my hair." "Jimmy pushed me." "Johnny sat in my seat." Once she realized this was a never-ending battle, she placed a tape recorder at her desk and taught the kids how to press the pause button, speak into the recorder, and press the pause again when they were done.

She promised to listen to their complaints at the end of the day. At first, when they would come to her, she had to remind them to use the recorder. But after a few days, the kids would go straight to the machine that would validate their feelings. Sometimes a line would form, and she would have to send them back to their desks, but for the most part, it worked flawlessly.

Occasionally, she would listen to the messages and have a wonderful chuckle. The children felt their needs were met because they could express their complaints and know they would be heard. That's all they needed. That release. That validation that justice would be served.

Don't take this the wrong way, but some of y'all need a tape recorder. Too many gripes. If you are constantly complaining and focusing on the negatives, just get yourself a recorder or a journal. Try processing that stuff on your own before bringing it into the world.

I'm not saying to bury your feelings, but be selective and find outlets to help you process them independently. People may like you a lot more. Journaling is a fantastic way to do this. Sometimes just getting it out of your mind and body helps. If someone specific is bothering you, write them a letter. You don't have to send it. In fact, you can burn it if you prefer, but getting it out helps the healing begin. They don't have to be part of your healing—you can do it all on your own. Become the driver and take control of your healing.

When I was a new mom, all the way until I was an old mom, random people seemed to want to give me parenting advice. All. The. Time. At first, it bothered me. I questioned my own maternal judgment. But after a few years, and after gaining confidence in my mothering skills, I learned to simply say, "Thank you for your concern." It validated their feelings, as I'm sure they thought they were helping, and it gave me something to respond with automatically so I could process their advice later. I allowed them to feel heard, but I didn't allow myself to react quickly without thought. I would have time to digest their comment and decide if I would receive it or swipe it away.

Since then, every time I meet a new or expectant mother, I always tell them, "I only have one piece of advice for you"... they usually smile that 'Oh, here it comes' smile, which I recognize, and then I proceed to tell them, "Don't listen to any advice from anyone. Trust that you alone will know what's best for your child." It always ends with a huge smile and a sigh of relief.

For my well-being, I need to spend time in silence with my thoughts, time at yoga, and time spent in nature or with my family and friends. My time is important to me. I gave my time for decades, now I claim it back for myself as much as possible, and I do not feel bad about it. Remember, others cannot make you feel anything. You are the only one who does that.

I love to lay in my hammock under our oak tree in the backyard. I love to feel the wind, hear my mother's wind chimes gently bumping, and watch the ripples on the retention pond in our yard, which I admiringly call Peace Lake. Bailey, my little chihuahua mix, lovingly lays there with me. He lets me hold him like a little baby, and he'll look up into my eyes... Okay, okay, enough.

My point is that it doesn't have to be some huge thing to feel connected to your vibration. It just takes awareness. Stillness. And again, perspective. It's easy to cut corners with yourself, giving all your time to those you love or the obligations you feel passionate about. But too much of this can leave you feeling defeated and empty. Sometimes it's hard to stand your ground and make time for you. Choose yourself often enough so you don't lose sight of what makes you happy. Be the captain, the driver of your life.

You know when you're around certain people, and you just feel more alive? The food tastes better, you laugh harder, and you just enjoy yourself more? Those people have a similar vibration, or at least your vibrations meld well together. Same with the opposite. Sometimes when you're around someone, they might drain you. It's not that you don't like them—heck, sometimes you might even love them. It could be a family member, or a parent, even. But they leave you feeling empty, defeated, and drained.

You might find yourself taking deep breaths or needing some alone time when you break away from them. It's not that they're bad for you—it's just that your vibrations are different, and you have to work a little harder to enjoy them. They can be worth the effort, though. Maybe they're high-energy or super chill compared to you, depending on who they are and how they relate to you. You might have a lesson to learn with them or through them. Again, only you know the answers.

It's worth beating to a different drum for some people, but not for everyone. It's the process of learning who you are and what is best for you. Enjoy the learning.

TAKE THE WHEEL OF YOUR LIFE AND DRIVE.

PRACTICE *makes* POSITIVE

How Do We Get There?

GET HEALTHY

The most valuable thing in your life is your health. You could be married to the love of your life, holding the winning Powerball ticket, and writing lyrics like Taylor Swift, but if you're sick, you can't enjoy any of it. So, I'm going to ask you to start here: Get healthy. I don't care where you're located, or how much time or money you have, every single person reading this book can improve their health. Move more, eat less, drink less alcohol, take fewer prescription or non-prescription drugs, or simply eat your vegetables. Consult a doctor, a personal trainer, a health coach—whatever it is you need to get started.

You can even start by walking more. Even if you're a single parent with two small babies at home, you can walk a half block in one direction and then half a block in the other, while they nap in their crib. Take the baby monitor and go as far as it will reach, so you can be back to them quickly. (Dear Lord, don't let this get me in trouble... obviously, make sure your babies are safe!) Better yet, take them in the stroller and go for long walks after work. It will make you feel better. I promise.

Try different workouts. Your particular body and mind will absolutely despise some, tolerate others, and actually enjoy a few. For me, the one I dislike most is a spin class. I tolerate weights, mainly because I know I need to build muscle, but I don't do them as much as I probably should. I actually enjoy yoga, Pilates, and a nice walk with my husband and our pups. So those are the ones I focus on. You can find any workout on YouTube and do it right from your home. Again, if nothing else, walk. Do what you can for this phase or time in your life.

I ran for twenty years because I had a busy household and not a lot of extra money for workouts. I could run anywhere, at any time of day, and it only took thirty minutes. I usually chose to run before the house woke up, and all I really needed was a decent pair of running shoes. With small children, this also became my quiet time. It was where I spent time with my thoughts. Later, when I found a running partner, it became therapy time. We even named it "run club" because what was discussed in run club never left run club.

I can also say there's something even more therapeutic when you can discuss your thoughts while doing something physical. It helps process them faster and deeper when you're mentally and physically challenged at the same time. Plus, you can always blame the tears on sweat, if need be. Exercise not only changes your body, but it also changes your mind, attitude, and mood—and that will inevitably change your life.

Except for those with a medical condition, please stop being a germaphobe. This leads to feelings of "the world is out to get me." I'm not saying go lick the inside of a garbage can, but stop being afraid to live or interact with people because you're scared you'll touch a germ. You're creating an invisible barrier between yourself and others.

I know, if you're reading this and you're a germaphobe, you're probably thinking, "GOOD, that's the intention!"

However, feeling disconnected over time will not serve you well. Being afraid to interact with people or leave your home can lead to isolation. These feelings of germ paranoia can grow until they're no longer controllable, leading to true, uncontrollable isolation. There are people who become unable to leave their home. I'm not saying this will happen to you, but just be mindful.

Don't miss out on life because of fear. You're wasting positive energy and creating negative thoughts. People pick up on your vibration—they feel your fear and avoidance. You need community. You need to connect with others. Germs and all.

Your healthy body is strong enough to be exposed to things and fight them off. It improves your immunity and can actually make you stronger and healthier. Sometimes, your mental health takes precedence over your physical health, and community is essential for your mental well-being. Obviously, if you have a compromised immune system or underlying health issues, this does not apply to you.

Next, stretch. Lay on the floor of your bedroom and put your arms in a T-shape, then move your knees from side to side. Bend over and touch your toes. Reach your hands above your head and lean from side to side. Search YouTube for stretching sequences. Feel your body changing, reaching, stretching, and moving. And then be thankful for that feeling.

When we are children, we can move in so many ways. Touching our toes is as easy as breathing, but as we age, we slowly lose certain stretching abilities. By the time we're elderly, it can be difficult to get back to the level we once were. So, do what you can to maintain the flexibility you have now for as long as possible. This will help you age well and keep you moving longer. Flexibility is an easy thing to lose—it sneaks up on you—but it's much harder to regain. Never give up on stretching. It's so important.

Eat better. Less processed food, more fruits and vegetables, less sugar. Just try to be mindful of what and how much you're consuming. Still eat what you love, but maybe have less of the unhealthy stuff and more of the good stuff.

Prioritize your health because nothing matters more. Like they told us in Sunday school, your body is your temple. You only get one, and it will treat you as well as you treat it. It will only last as long as the regular maintenance you provide it. It's your vessel for this life. Without it... well, you know what happens, and you don't want to rush that.

Sleep better. I should probably start with a disclaimer: I'm a pretty good sleeper. I fall asleep fast and can stay asleep all night (except for my 4 a.m. potty break). I can sleep in a car, a plane, a train, or even during a long enough red light. So, take this chapter as you wish.

When I have trouble staying asleep, it's usually because I'm anxious or excited about something. When I was starting my business or writing this book, I would wake up and work. Some of my best thoughts came at night. Speaking of anxiousness and excitement, I once heard that both feelings are the same—same chemical and neurological reactions in your body. The only difference is perception. Your brain perceives them differently based on the environment. I don't know if it's true, but ever since I heard this, whenever I or one of my kids is anxious about something, I remind myself and them that we're actually feeling excited. We're simply excited for the opportunity in front of us. We feel the opportunity for growth presenting itself, which creates excitement, not anxiousness.

Just a reminder here: This book is not meant to treat any form of clinically diagnosed mental illness. Also, I'm not trying to diminish extreme or uncontrolled thoughts or behaviors. Remember, this is simply an insight into my brain and how it works.

Back to sleep cycles. It's my personal opinion that we spend way too much time in artificial light. Our homes are filled with light bulbs that manipulate our bodies' natural sleep rhythms. We are truly tricking our brains into staying awake and alert by disguising the darkness. We look at laptops, phones, televisions—we even read on tablets with ambient light. Let your body see and feel the sunshine and the darkness. Open the blinds of your home. Go outside. Let your brain know what time of day it is.

Especially at night, if you're having a hard time sleeping, go outside. Let your mind and body experience the darkness. Sit in silence. Let your brain slow down. We sit in so much artificial light that I worry our brains no longer understand natural sleep cycles. You flip the light switch off and expect your brain to switch off. But if you've been going a million miles a minute during the day, how does your brain know to suddenly shift into sleep mode? A transition into quiet and natural lighting might help. If it's not safe where you live to go outside at night, sit by a window and look at the night sky. Try to find a window that avoids streetlights and noise, if possible.

The hardest part is trying not to get frustrated with sleeplessness. This is literally an internal fight with yourself. Try to accept it, sit with it, and take micro steps to address it. Find out what your mind is trying to tell you. Give yourself silence during the day, so you can get to know that feeling and call upon it at night. Channel the moments of silence, harness the stillness, and learn to use it to shut your mind off when it's time for quiet.

If you've tried the darkness and quiet route, maybe there's something else going on. Perhaps your brain can't find its natural vibration and is trying to tell you something. Maybe something inside of you desperately wants to come out, but you're so far away from knowing who you are and what you want—your vibration—that your brain is frustrated.

Your brain will speak to you. It will shut you down if it needs to. That's why people pass out, faint, have a seizure, or even experience mini strokes. When your body and mind feel off, they will let you know. Shingles is another side effect of stress, along with headaches—and of course, sleepless nights. These are all signs that your body and mind are out of rhythm. Your vibration is off. It's better for you to address it before your mind takes over, shutting you down or keeping you from sleep.

Your thoughts will play around in your consciousness and unconsciousness, hoping to get through to you. Hoping to be heard. Hoping to shake things up a little.

I know so many people who struggle with sleep, and I wish I could do more to help. I honestly think it goes back to the idea that if you don't feel good—physically or mentally— nothing else really matters.

You are the only one who can make getting healthy a priority, but this is the start of everything. You must feel better to change anything else. This is absolutely the most important step. You cannot improve any other part of your life without first feeling better. Sleeping better will give you more energy and help you have a better outlook on life. If you have aches and pains, or simply low energy, you won't be receptive to new things. You won't have the energy for them. So, we need to fix the way you feel physically before we can work on how you feel mentally.

Secondly, love your body. Every day, be thankful for your body. Look yourself in the mirror and tell yourself, "I am thankful for my body. I am thankful for my strong, beautiful, and healthy body." (Thanks, Adriene!) No matter what your body looks like, feels like, or moves like, it's the only one you're going to get, so you'd better get used to it and learn to love it. Even if you have some physical limitations, this is you. This is your starting point. This has to be okay. We can't change it; we can only improve from our individual starting point.

LOVE YOURSELF

Once you start getting healthier and stronger, be proud of your mind and body for getting you there. Be thankful for the baby steps, the micro-improvements. They will add up. Give yourself time to get back to where you need to be, where you can be. Don't be too hard on yourself. If you fail, just start again. Be thankful for the power and control you have over your choices. Recognize the good ones and celebrate them. Recognize the bad ones and swipe them away. Don't let the negativity take over. Acknowledge it and let it go.

You must love yourself before anyone else can love you. You can truly only love yourself if you feel like you're doing the best you can. Only you know what that level is. You are the only one who can truly hold yourself accountable, for you're the only one who knows your best ability.

Self-loathing comes from negative thoughts you tell yourself. It comes from within. It's you not living up to your own expectations and not being kind to yourself. It's an internal battle between you and yourself. It's crazy to think that we can be our own worst enemy sometimes. The good news is, we can learn a whole new internal dialogue. We can learn to like ourselves more, treat ourselves better. We can learn to be the best we want to be. We're in control of the outcome. We can do the things we enjoy. We can create happiness. We choose our paths, our thoughts. We choose what we prioritize, what we value, and we choose our emotions and what we allow into our minds. You can train your brain to simply swipe away what you don't want. Close that browser altogether! Practice choosing.

Sometimes, when it all builds up to the point of breaking, you cannot swipe it away. During certain times of our lives, it will just feel like you're being thrown too much all at once. We question just how much more we can take. The car won't start, your child missed the bus, you forgot your laptop, your mom needs you to pick up her prescription, your spouse is complaining about... something, and the dog ran away. It's all coming at once, and you might feel like you're about to break.

If you're someone who spends their day filling everyone's cup and running around ragged, then on days like this, I give you permission to stop. Just stop. Let it all happen. Whatever is going to fall, let it fall. When you can't fix it all, don't fix any of it. When you can't do it all, don't do any of it. Just for one day. Just take one day off and sit outside. Seriously. If you're an overachiever who handles it all, one day won't matter. Trust me, it will all wait for you to do it tomorrow, but give yourself a day to recover, rejuvenate, and the time to prioritize what's really important. Take a mental health day and do nothing. Taking a break will give you clarity. Just make a cup of tea or your favorite beverage and go outside and sit in silence. Also, your loved ones might back off just a bit; they might even pitch in and help a little too.

Next, I would like you to sit taller, walk with your shoulders back, and your head tilted slightly up. You are God's creation—walk around like you are a masterpiece. Smile more.

Not only does this trick your mind into feeling better, but the world will also receive you better. People will smile back. Strangers may open doors for you and ask how your day is going. Do the same for others. Let cars merge in front of you, hold the door open for someone, make eye contact, and smile. You'll be so surprised by what strong posture and a smile can do for your day.

Interact with the world as you walk through it. Feel the sun, feel the breeze, feel the vibrations of the people walking by. See how they change when you smile and look at them. Look for things that make you happy: your favorite color, a flower, a cute baby, a nicely dressed person. Have your internal dialogue speak to you. For example: "That's a cute dog. She looks nice. Oh, that person made eye contact. That person smiled back. That bird's song sounds pretty. I feel taller when I hold my shoulders back. I'm so happy I chose a healthy breakfast this morning. I made my first good decision of the day. I love this song. Today will be a good day. I can already feel it." Train your brain to point out the good things, and then tell yourself what they are.

"Give every day the chance to become the most beautiful day of your life."

—Mark Twain

For some of you, this might be easy. For others, it might take some practice. Here are a few examples of negative thoughts: "I can't believe I woke up late. I really wanted pancakes this morning, but I had boiled eggs instead, eggs are gross. Stupid diets. They never work anyway. Look at her, she looks nice. I don't have anything that looks good on me. My clothes are old, and I'm so out of shape. Come on, lady, get your dog across the road. I'm going to be late as it is." If your thoughts go more like this, we've got some work to do.

You're already making your brain want to check out. You're making me want to check out. Your mannerisms are probably closed off, and your expressions are probably negative at best. You're probably very unapproachable, grumpy even. Your vibration is dark, negative, and borderline toxic. You will have a bad day because you're only focusing on what you don't like, what you don't have, and what you perceive you're doing wrong or missing out on.

Even if you don't want to be around you. You probably just want to go numb, turning off all thoughts because they're not good ones. Well, let's practice stopping the bad thoughts and learning to incorporate the good thoughts. When you catch yourself being negative or harmful to your happiness, stop right there and change the words. Practice makes positive.

TRY NEW THINGS

You can train your brain to reevaluate everything you see. You can search out the good things and start a mental dialogue there. It will take daily practice to break the negative habits you've already created. Trying new paths and creating new connections can make it easier.

Try things that excite you, things that you never thought were available to you. If you fall or fail, laugh about it! You are meant to experience life and all that you want to do. You are not meant to succeed at everything, and you certainly are not meant to be the best at everything. But it's okay to try, to have fun, and be totally bad at it. Just try it on and see how it fits. My husband and I went country line dancing once, and we were the worst! But we laughed and poked fun at ourselves. Others went out of their way to help teach us. We had a great time and would go again, even though it was totally embarrassing. No one assumed we would be great at it, including ourselves. You should not be great at anything new. That is normal.

You may love it, you may hate it, but you can say, "Yeah, I tried that once!" The more you try, the happier you'll feel, even if you're not good at it. Your mind, body, and soul want to grow and experience life to the fullest. It's self-doubt that keeps you from it, and you are the one in control of that. Let that go.

Trying new things will show you a lot that you are not good at, but it will also show you the things you are good at. The things you never even knew you would love. The things you can have confidence and pride in doing. The things that fill your cup and make your vibration vibe brighter! You never know until you try them. It may take a little practice too. My daughter just came home and told me she wrote a three-minute speech in twenty minutes. Last year, it took her months to write a three-minute speech, but with time and practice, it's much easier now. The more we do things, the easier they get.

Since my children were little, I always asked them to give me experiences instead of gifts. When they were young, I would ask them to play with my hair, try new food with me, or maybe just sit outside with me and talk. They would feel so much pride in these gifts because it truly came from them. It came from their ideas and thoughts of what I might enjoy. Plus, they got to join in the enjoyment too.

Later in life, this transitioned into some amazing activities. I've been taken to glassblowing classes, painting classes, ceramic bowl making, facials, lunches, electric boating adventures, picnics in the park, and have done some pretty crazy adventure ropes courses. Not only is it a great bonding experience, but we also try new things that we might have never tried! I absolutely love it. Also, none of it is crazy expensive—it just takes some research. Groupon usually has great options in your local area.

STAY FOCUSED ON YOUR DREAM

Pay attention to your course, your path. This is your life—the only one you're going to get. You need to be in control of it. You need to know what you want, where you want to go, and when to change course, take action, or sit still for a moment and check in with your progress. Try not to get stuck for too long, and always think about not only today but your five-, ten-, and fifteen-year projections. You will get to where you plan to go. If you fail to plan, you leave your destiny up to everyone and everything but you.

Now trust me, I've birthed five babies. I get that there are plenty of days when you're raising children that you don't get to choose anything that happens to you. Heck, you can't even choose to get a shower sometimes, but you can look ahead one year, five years, and ten years. You must have a dream and a plan to get there. Patiently plan for the things your heart desires.

I also understand that plans can take a little longer to achieve than you might want, but micro-movements in the right direction will get you there. Practice consistency and repetition. Practice daily, or at least weekly, check-ins with yourself. Am I where I need to be? Am I happy with the things I'm doing? Am I feeling happy? Am I pleased with my vibration?

When I was in college, I wanted to teach elementary school. Kindergarten through second grade was my dream age group, but I went into sales because, at the time, I thought I needed to make more money than teaching could provide.

I put my dream of teaching on hold to support my family, but that never meant my dream of teaching went away. It also didn't mean that I didn't find happiness in my other career. To the contrary! I loved sales. I loved meeting new people, taking care of clients, and making their jobs easier. I also loved winning awards and competitions and beating sales goals. It was my season to be in sales, while my dream of teaching waited on the sidelines.

FOLLOW HAPPINESS

Do not follow money, follow happiness. This does not mean you should run out on your responsibilities. If you must work two jobs to support your kids, do it. If you must work full-time while attending college full-time, do it. Whatever you must do to get through to the other side, do it. Make sure you are responsible in your thinking and planning so you don't end up in a predicament. But during that time, also make plans for your dreams. If you plan, you will get there. Just keep taking micro-steps in that direction.

Now that my children are older and we have a little nest egg, I still want to teach. I am currently applying for all teaching positions near my home that have an opening for K-6. I'm scared to death. I have no idea how to run a classroom. But what the heck, why not?! I want to know that at the end of my life, I checked all the boxes for the things I wanted to do and try. This brings me to my next point: follow happiness.

I will be fifty-three in August, and I may become a first-time teacher next school year. I just took the long way—or scenic route—to get here. You have nothing but time, and you can do all the things you want to do with a little planning. You just have to want to do it badly enough. Following your happiness will get you there.

Never, ever think it's too late or that you are too old to try something new or follow your passions. If anything, now is the only time left. Don't let what others might think or say stop you either. This is your life to live how you want to live it. Let them talk and speculate away. At least you are giving them something to talk about!

Although you may need a nest egg to make your dreams happen, wealth does not equate to happiness. Money can make things easier, but it can also complicate things. Happiness is an emotion that cannot be purchased. When you love your life, money can come and money can go, but your happiness should remain regardless. If you are living within your true self and your true vibration, happiness will be abundant.

I once read that we are the only living animal that pays to live on the earth. That was mind-blowing to me. We feel the need to buy things, and once we've purchased something, we want the next thing, the better thing. But guess what? No matter what you buy, there is a better or newer thing out there. You will never, ever, ever fill that cup of desire. But if you love the things you already have, you will be happy. Really, we need so little. We need shelter, food/water, love, and community. Everything else is just stuff. Stuff gets old. Stuff breaks. Stuff is heavy. A life in full vibration is much better than stuff.

Spend more time outside. Sit on your front porch, your back porch, your neighbor's porch—just go. Go for walks, sit under a tree, lay in the grass in your yard or in Central Park. Just go outside. GO. Go outside at different times of the day. Find out which one you like the best: sunrise, sunset, midnight, or the heat of the day when the sunshine is the brightest. Maybe you like all of them! Lay down and look at the stars one night. Listen to the animals and the noises they make. Connect with nature and the world around you. Experience the beauty of the world. Soak it in and make it part of you.

We spend too much time in unnatural light with the blinds closed. We are meant to be in nature, roaming, stretching, running. We are meant to be in sunlight. Ten minutes a day is all you really need, but you do need it. You can combine it with your mindfulness and spending time with your thoughts. Are you worth ten minutes a day? The answer is yes! Yes, you are!

Any time in my life that I had a baby or child who could not get settled, all I had to do was walk outside with them, and almost immediately the tears would stop. When they seemed to be climbing the walls and driving me crazy, we would go play outside. Whenever I wanted to really bond with them and enjoy their laughter, we would go outside. Whenever I needed community, we would go outside. Whenever I needed to not see the messy house, we would go outside.

Sometimes, after dinner, we would go outside. Neighbors would come out, and before we knew it, hours would go by. We would go in, and it would be time for baths and bed, but no one complained. It seems on those nights, they were full of life and love. They were content and ready to sleep.

Go outside. Talk to people. Now... go. I kid, keep reading, but maybe sit on a chair in your driveway with the book. Seriously, please spend a lot more time outside. It will change everything.

I have mentioned my dad a few times in this book. Now, let me tell you a little about what my mom taught me. She taught me to find joy in every day, to celebrate everything, to love to your highest ability, and to fight for yourself and your children more than anything else. She loved life and her people more than anything in the world.

When she was in the last few years of her life, I would witness how music would bring her back to her happiness. She loved listening to the oldies and the sing-along songs, or the old country classics that would coax a tear or two. It just brought her right back to her younger days. If there was a live musician around, this really got her going. She would dance in her seat, and her face would just light up. Music is so important to our lives. It is like a time stamp of history. It takes you to a time in your life and pulls those memories and feelings right back to the surface. So, listen to a lot of different kinds of music in different parts of your day or life. Ignite those feelings, create those memories. They will be fun to relive later when you might need them the most.

We spend so much time numbing ourselves. Numbing ourselves with food, drink, recreational drugs, prescription drugs, binge-watching TV, working, playing video games—whatever it is that pulls you away from you. When we do this, we are numbing our vibration. Our minds might be stimulated artificially, but our hearts and bodies have succumbed to numbness. You are not living your best life if you are doing this daily. Again, go outside, listen to music, find community, find what stimulates you. Find who you are again.

Children need nothing of the sort to be happy—nothing artificial. They run, they play, they become best friends with strangers, they laugh, they spin around, they color, they play make-believe, and they daydream. That child still lives inside of you. She has simply forgotten how to express herself.

ASKING AND GIVING

Do not be afraid to ask for things. If you have an expired coupon, ask if they will still take it. If your dentist cannot get you in for six months, ask if there is a waiting list for any cancellations. If someone you know has a job that can help you, ask for help. It's okay to ask. Now, don't be mean, and don't over-ask the same person for things, but a little 'lean-in' is totally fine.

Make sure you do it with a smile. It actually makes some people happy to help. It builds friendships. It can make that person feel proud. It makes people feel closer. Be sure to reciprocate the favor whenever possible and never take advantage of people or a situation. If it's big enough to ask, give a thank-you note or gift.

Always buy from someone starting a business. You do not need to spend more than you can afford, but if someone starts a home business, help them out that first month. You do not need to continue to buy if you do not like or need the product, but you can usually find something to buy to support a friend's new venture. Same with any kid on a corner selling lemonade. Buy a cup and pay twice what they are asking. It feels good to make someone's day and encourage their dreams. It is amazing how many people remember their first customer and always appreciate the kindness shown.

Do not take offense so easily. Other people's opinions are just that—opinions. If you are living in your own vibration, then you really should not care too much. If someone says something you do not agree with, just shake it off. Allow them to have their voice and their opinion and respect it. This may take a bit of practice, but you know the drill by now. Practice makes positive.

Remember, it is better to respond than to react, and sometimes it is better to not speak at all. Do not use your energy on anger or worry. Use your energy to make you a better person. Use your energy to grow, to love, to trust, to create, to shine, and beat in vibration.

Treat yourself. Do not wait for other people to make you happy. Find things you enjoy and do them daily. My grandmother used to sweep her front porch every day at 4:00. Afterwards, she would come inside, fill a glass with ice— I mean, to the very top. Then she would take a glass Coke bottle out of the fridge. It had to be glass. She would pour that

Coke over the ice ever so slowly. She would wait for the bubbles to stop popping, then she would take the smallest sip. She would hold the liquid in her mouth for a brief moment, with her eyes closed, and smile. Then when she swallowed, she would open her eyes and make a sound, opening her mouth. *Ahhhhhhhhh.* She would open her eyes and look at me and say, "Now this is a treat well earned."

She did this every day, and it taught me to enjoy the small things, treat yourself after putting in the hard work, and don't wait for others to provide these moments for you, or even for them to join in. This was her private, special moment she did every day just for herself.

For one of my birthdays, I planned a little weekend getaway at a nearby local bed and breakfast in a small suburb. I wanted to walk to everything and spend the day sampling local cuisine and browsing in the small shops. I told my husband that the only thing I wanted for my birthday was for him to join me in this adventure and not complain—not once. In fact, it was literally one of the best weekends. It also helps that our birthdays are 13 days apart, so we celebrate together.

When we were first married, he asked me to tell him what I wanted. He said he would do anything he needed to do to make me happy, but that he would never be able to read my mind or pick up on any hints. It just was not his strong suit. So, this is what we do. I plan and he smiles. It is great! He does still surprise me sometimes, and when he does plan something, it is amazing. If you want to do something, do it. Invite your spouse first, but if they do not want to come, bring a friend, a neighbor, or a child. Do not get angry. Do not pout. Do not put expectations for your happiness on others.

DON'T WORRY, JUST DO YOU

It's senseless to worry about things that are out of your control. There are some things that are just either going to happen or they are not. The only thing you can do is be prepared for the worst, but do not let worry consume you. If you cannot do anything to change the outcome, just let it be. For example, you probably aren't going to solve world hunger, create world peace, or prevent war, so go ahead and live your life to the best of your ability. Now, if you think you can fix one of those things, by all means, please do. The rest of us would appreciate it.

But just like those things, you cannot control if your company gets bought out or if your best friend must move. Things are going to happen sometimes that are not worth the worry if you cannot change the outcome anyway. Do not waste your energy on things out of your control. This will take a bit of practice if you are accustomed to worrying, but breaking this habit and retraining your brain will be so worth the effort.

FOCUS ON THE GOOD

Find a spot in your home that is special to you and make it all you can imagine. I once bought a $15 plastic pink chandelier and put it in my laundry room. I loved it! When I had five children in the home, I spent a lot of time doing laundry, and I wanted to make it pretty. I put some family pictures in there, and the ceramic projects my kids would bring home from school. I did this so when I was there, I would feel blessed that I was lucky enough to have kids for whom I could do laundry and be thankful that they had nice clothes to wear.

I hung a picture of my grandmother in there too. I did this so if I ever felt annoyed with laundry, I would remember her hanging laundry on a clothesline in her backyard, where she would share stories with me about how she washed on a washboard when she was my age. It's really all about remembering how good you have it. There is always someone who has it better, and there is always someone who has it worse.

Make a reading corner, a prayer pillow by your bed, a yoga corner in your spare bedroom, a bench under a tree in your backyard, a bathtub surrounded by plants and candles—just find a small space in or around your home and add things that make you happy.

Visit that space daily and know that you can go there and feel calm. Let this be a place where you take a cup of tea, a book, or simply go and just sit. Where you just listen. Maybe close your eyes or listen to some music or nature.

Train your brain and muscles that this place, and this moment, is just about connecting with yourself. Train your family, when they see you sitting there, to maybe hold their questions for a few moments. Take time to sit there for ten minutes before the kids come home from school, ten minutes before the house wakes up, or maybe ten minutes before you go to bed. Make the place, even if you do not have time in your day for it yet. At least you can walk by it and see it and know, eventually, you will be there. Share the space with your loved ones too. Let them touch it, feel it, and experience it, but make sure they respect the space. Maybe help them create a space of their own too. You can even let them catch you enjoying their space as well. You will be amazed to see their faces light up when they know you like their special place. What a beautiful message.

Another way to focus on the good is to find moments throughout your day to sprinkle in happiness. I like to make Sunday breakfast a little more special. I play Sunday brunch music and make a unique spread of food. If I make pancakes, I do not just serve plain pancakes and syrup. I make blueberry pancakes with topping options, such as powdered sugar and whipped cream. If I make waffles, I set out fruit topping options. I cut up bananas and strawberries, putting them in separate bowls for serving. I make it more of a buffet, kind of a make-your-own-waffle station.

For years, every Christmas, I would add a little ground cinnamon to the coffee grinds before brewing. Just a little sprinkle on top. About 12 years in, my husband looked at me one Christmas morning and said, "The coffee just seems to taste better on Christmas morning." I just smiled and said, "Must be the Christmas magic." It's just fun to add a little something special to the ordinary. It elevates the simple.

When my older kids came home from school, I would have snacks cut up and placed in fancy dishes at the table to encourage them to sit with me and tell me about their day.

To my surprise and delight, once I started working, they would do the same for me. I would walk into the house to candlelight, soft jazz, and them waiting with cheese and crackers to hear about my day. It's really the little things in life that can connect us the most.

Do not buy too much. Less is always more. Buying things gives you an instant rush of joy and excitement, but that feeling is so temporary. Buying things will not only clutter your home, it will deplete your funds that could be used to make memories. Just ask yourself if you really need it or if it just makes sense in the moment. Less is always more. Maybe start saving the money you would have spent. Put it in a sock drawer, and at the end of six months, notice how much you saved, then take a long weekend and go somewhere to make memories with that money. It's amazing to see how much money we waste on things we do not even notice or remember. Dave Ramsey, a money savings guru we like, suggests carrying cash so you can really feel every purchase. Only spend the cash you set aside to waste.

THE GIFT OF LISTENING

Take time to talk to the older generation. They have a slowness about them that is so peaceful. I do not mean slowness because they are old, but slowness because they grew up in a different time. The world moved slower, people talked slower, and they spent way more time in face-to-face communities. They have the best expressions, eye contact, and detail for every emotion. They speak with the most detailed descriptions. They make the best storytellers.

Maybe this does not hold true for relatives in your own family, but when you meet an older person on a walk, they love to share their stories with those who have never heard them before. They light up, and they seem to have such poetry in their words. You might learn a thing or two, but if nothing else, it will feel like the noise and hustle and bustle of your own life goes away for a few minutes.

We have this older woman in our neighborhood. She will stand on the sidewalk and wave to every car that goes by with the enthusiasm of Forrest Gump. She always has the biggest smile, the best posture, and the kindest energy. If you are walking by her, she will bless you, compliment you, sing to you, or tell you just how fabulous you are doing. She might tell you how beautiful your family is or talk about what a stupendous day it is today. When you are near her, you cannot help but feel happiness. Now, she will talk to you for as long as you stand there, but while you are with her, you cannot help but feel her glorious vibration. Everyone in the neighborhood knows who she is. She is out there for at least four hours a day, simply spreading love.

These are the kind of people who amaze me. They touch so many people throughout their lifetime. They seem to give without running out of giving. They never blend in. Their light never seems to dim. They always have enough energy for their own lives, and then still an overpouring amount of energy for the rest of the world too. It is a never-ending outpouring of energy, love, and kindness. They never seem to need to recharge. Sometimes I wonder if they are angels just spending time down here in the real world, spreading love and shining light on us. The gift of listening is a two-way gift. It gives joy to the giver and the receiver.

COMPLIMENTS ARE MAGIC

Compliment people. It makes you feel good, and it makes them feel good. If you think of something nice, say it. If you like someone, look for something nice to say. "I love that hat. You have the prettiest smile. You always seem to have the right thing to say. I admire the way you parent. I appreciate you." If you are looking for things to compliment someone you love, then you will have happy thoughts about the person you love. You will also see positive things as a byproduct, and you will be happier too.

It does not take much to make someone smile. If you are thinking about it, and it's nice, say it. If you like the person even better, but do not stop there—compliment a stranger. Leave a kind note in your mailbox for the mail person, maybe compliment their daily punctuality. Tell your child's teacher they are doing an excellent job. Tell your spouse they made you feel special today. Thank your teenager for making a desirable choice. You can even tell your mother-in-law that you enjoyed her Sunday dinner. Planting seeds of kindness and sprinkling compliments around brightens not only your life but others' lives as well. Plus, the flowers they grow are beautiful.

No one is better than you. We all have our specialness. There are people who are smarter. There are people who are more talented. There are people who are stronger, richer, better looking, and funnier. Okay, okay, you get it, I know. But guess what? There are also others who are less strong, less rich, less good looking, and less funny. You are just exactly where you are meant to be with exactly the right amount of special sauce that is meant for you.

Appreciate what you have, celebrate others for what they have, and focus on your own special vibration, and how it best fits into the world around you. You are the only one that is uniquely you. You are the only one who makes your sound. Your life is yours for the making. Do not let anyone convince you differently. Would you go to a restaurant and order something you do not like? No!

DON'T LIVE A LIFE YOU DON'T LOVE.

The 1 & 10 Moments

When people are living what I like to call the 1 and 10 moments, their feelings are heightened, and the friendship you extend during those times means so much more. So, what are the 1 and 10 moments? It's the moments people remember. It derives from the scale of 1 to 10—1 being the worst and 10 being the best. These are the moments that define who you are. They mold you. Most of life falls in the 4 to 6 categories—the everyday. Nothing too good, nothing too bad. Maybe you missed your favorite show. Maybe you got a front-row parking spot. Nothing horrible, but nothing amazing. It's simply normal life. Nothing stands out too much. Nothing happens that you will remember for long. I call these the filler days. Someone might say, "What did you do this weekend?" and you can't remember because it was a 4 to 6 kind of weekend.

Numbers 2 and 3 are more somber, low points. Maybe your boss was upset because you lost a project or sale you were working hard on. Maybe you fought with your spouse, or your child was hurt by a friend. It's bad enough that you may cry or need some quiet time, but life goes on normally. Your routine may change a little these days. You may choose to run a bath versus watch TV with the family. Maybe you call your mom to vent about the day. Something happened to make you sad or feel bad about where you are. It's a personal low, but more than likely tomorrow you will wake up feeling better.

Days or moments that feel like a 7, 8, and 9 are on the happy side. You closed the sale. Your fantasy football team won. Something you've been wanting or dreaming about may have happened. Your best friend is coming to visit. Your spouse made your favorite meal. Maybe you won $20 on a scratch-off ticket. Whatever it is, you feel good and like everything is going your way. Just good, happy stuff. The things that make your heart happy and your vibration hum. You might go out to dinner to celebrate. You might call your dad to share the good news. These are really good days, yet not necessarily days you will remember in a few years. They are way better than filler days, just not life-altering.

Then there are the 1 and 10 moments. These are the really big ones. These are the moments that take you to your knees. These moments stop time. These moments you never forget. These memories come back to you in full color. You can see the people who were there. You can feel the emotions you felt by just remembering. These moments hit you deep in the gut. Sometimes these moments happen in our personal lives, but sometimes they happen to our entire nation or world. A global pandemic. The day those planes hit the World Trade Center on 9/11. The day Kennedy was shot. The day Princess Diana died. The day Kobe Bryant died. The day the space shuttle blew up. These are all the 1's we can remember. We remember who we were with. We remember what we were doing when the news came. These moments connect us on such a deeper level. They connect us with strangers. They connect us as a nation. They mean something. We memorialize them.

In our personal lives, the 1's may be when a parent dies. A child dies. Someone we love is in the hospital, or there was a bad accident, and we don't know the outcome. A cancer diagnosis. These moments take our focus from everything normal and routine. We might feel like we can't breathe or go on. We lose the ability to think straight. Our bodies might go numb or run on autopilot. This is when we need others to guide us. We need to lean on others for support because we are too weak to stand on our own. We aren't sure how or when we will recover. We are broken, and time stands still. Heartbroken. The people who are there for us know us well; they know the situation. We never forget these moments and where we pulled our strength from.

Hopefully, for every 1 moment we have in life, it can be counterbalanced by a 10 moment. We can share these moments with our nation and possibly the world as well. The mask mandate being lifted! A Super Bowl victory. The first man to walk on the moon. The fall of the Berlin Wall. The capture of a really bad person. A war ending.

In our personal lives, the 10's can be a wedding. The birth of a child. A graduation. A loved one gets news that they are going to survive an accident or are cleared of cancer. These, again, are the moments that stop the normal day and any normal routine. The world is different these days. The air is different. Nothing else matters.

The people who show up for you on these days, the days that your world stops, are the ones you will remember. Those are your people. Those connections are unbreakable. You have now shared something that will always be immortalized. Even if you never see them again, they will always live within that memory of that event, and you will forever share an unbreakable bond.

Do the same for them. Be there for sickness, funerals, and losses. Sometimes when people experience a loss, they become so numb they do not know what they need or how to ask for help. Just sitting with them or walking next to them while they grieve is everything. Just help them cry. Make these moments in your loved ones' lives a priority. It will never be forgotten. They need you.

When your loved ones are going through these moments, it's hard to know exactly what to do, but helping them navigate through this time is what the connection is all about. It will bring you closer. They will feel the love much more deeply. It will connect you on a whole new level. The 1 and 10 moments of life are life. They are the moments you never forget. Your 1 and 10 people are everything. They say if you can name 5, you are truly blessed.

BIRTHRIGHT

Your life is your life. Some of us are born rich, some poor. Some are born into a family fortune or business, with a path clearly laid out—should they choose to take it. Some must figure things out in childhood because their parents were unable to care for them properly. Some must quit school to support their families. Some are born into environments of addiction. Some are born with natural talent that opens doors to fame and fortune. Some are born with disabilities. Some are born into hardworking families who live the American Dream. Whatever life you were born into—whatever challenges you face within your original nuclear family—that is your life. Your starting point. The one thing that cannot be changed.

There is nothing you can do about your birthright. Try not to compare your life to others, and instead, focus on making the most of the life you were given. There is a reason you have the life you have. You were given the tools you need to survive it. Your genetic code has been passed down through generations, evolving into you. You carry the best of your ancestry. It is your job to move it forward, to take steps that will benefit future generations.

Live your best 1 and 10 moments, and don't compare them to someone else's. You may be the first in your family to graduate high school, while your best friend was accepted to Harvard. Both are 10 moments.

Each of us should strive to be better than the generation before us—not better than our neighbors. It's like beating your own personal record rather than competing against your teammates. This mindset creates a healthier outlook and allows dreams and desires to unfold more naturally.

We all love to watch the stars of Hollywood—the lights, the glamour. But we're not necessarily jealous of them. In fact, we often live vicariously through them. Jealousy, on the other hand, is both ugly and useless. Nothing good ever comes from it. Some people may appear to have an endless string of 10-level moments, but believe me, they experience 1-level moments, too. Don't waste your energy on envy.

I recently read that most people can't name their great-grandparents. Just two generations—gone, forgotten. These are your parents' grandparents, the ones who likely came to America in search of a better life, who fought disease to survive, who endured loss yet carried on to build the foundation of your family tree. They faced famine, built homes with their bare hands, drank water from creeks. Every decision they made, every obstacle they overcame, every hardship they endured—each step brought them closer to your existence. And in their darkest moments, they likely imagined you. The life you would have. The opportunities you would see. It was probably those very hopes that carried them through.

Does knowing your great-grandchildren may not remember your name make you want to live differently? Does it push you to take more risks? To seize today's opportunities? Or does it inspire you to create a lasting legacy? What if your great-grandparents had gone south instead of west? How different would your life be?

What if the choices you make today could impact future generations? In my area, there are a few great-grandparents whose names everyone knows. Why? Because neighborhoods and communities are named after them. These families bought land—lots of it. They never benefited from it themselves. They simply served as stewards, managing it, paying taxes, protecting it for the future. They understood that while they might never see a return, their children's children would. And perhaps, just perhaps, their names would be remembered.

I don't know about you, but this realization makes me feel both completely insignificant and incredibly empowered. It calls me to live with more meaning, more conviction. Because while my name may one day fade, the impact of my choices does not.

TELL PEOPLE HOW YOU FEEL

If you don't tell people how you feel, how will they know? If you have important life events you want others to recognize, say something. How will they be aware of your feelings or what matters to you if you don't speak up? Some events are obvious, but others might need to be voiced.

Maybe you had a mammogram that came back suspicious, but after further testing, everything was fine. Celebrate that with someone you love! Ask a friend to lunch and tell them you have exciting news to share. This not only deepens your friendship but also gives you a chance to share your level 10 moments.

Human connection is important in all experiences, but those 1 and 10 moments? They're critical. We need them.

We assume others can see what we're going through, but our emotions, no matter how strong they feel on the inside, may not always show on the outside. If someone is crying, it's clear they're upset. But if they're quiet? You have no idea if they're happy, sad, tired, deep in thought, or just listening. You can ask how they are, but most people just respond with, "Fine."

So how can we really know?

The best way—say it. Tell people how you feel. Share your experiences. Now, I'm not saying you should break down in the checkout line at Marshalls when the cashier asks how your day is going, but be sure to tell your loved ones when you're not okay. Sometimes, we need a little help to get through.

When my kids were little, I let them struggle with things until they asked for help— simple things like a shape sorter, a puzzle, or putting on their shoes. One reason was to let them see if they could figure it out on their own. If they did, I'd cheer for them, and they loved it—especially because they often didn't realize I was watching.

Another reason? I wanted them to learn that in life, if you need help, you have to ask for it. No superhero is running around to save the day. Help doesn't just appear—you have to reach for it. They couldn't just whine or cry; they had to ask.

If they got frustrated or started to cry, I'd gently ask, "Would you like my help?" If they said yes, I'd help. Sometimes, they'd say no and try again. But if they still couldn't get it after a while, they'd ask in the sweetest voice, "Mommy, will you help me?" And I'd always reply, "Of course I will, my love. I'm glad you asked."

I believe this not only taught them to ask for help when they needed it, but also that there are people out there willing—no, happy—to help.

If you need help and don't have anyone to turn to, there are resources out there for you. Don't be afraid to look and ask. Start with a Google search. If you can't find what you need there, most employers have an HR department—Human Resources. HR exists to support the people in an organization, and what you share with them should be used to help you. If all else fails, ask a neighbor. Just ask. You don't have to suffer alone.

Only you truly know what you're feeling inside, what you can handle, and what's pushing you to your limit. Pay attention to when your tank is running low and find ways to refill it. But when you've completely run out of gas, you'd better push yourself to the nearest station—fast.

Again, we need community. We need connection. We need friendships. We need each other. If we constantly make others feel like their emotions and feelings don't matter, one day, we may look around and realize they're no longer there. I'm not saying you should live for others, but be mindful of the people you love. There's a balance—teetering between living your own truth and caring about others without caring too much about what they think of you. Daily check-ins and quiet moments of reflection help keep that balance.

Recently, I heard a response to "How are you?" that stopped me in my tracks. I was at the store, exchanging the usual polite greeting when the cashier's reply made me pause, look up, and smile. "I love that," I said. "May I use that moving forward?" She blushed and said, "Of course!"

Her response?

"Grateful."

Such a simple word, yet so powerful. It doesn't mean good or bad. It could mean grateful for a lesson just learned, grateful to have a job, grateful for a clean bill of health. Whatever the moment holds, it's a grateful moment.

So how am I? I am truly grateful.

Just beautiful.

WHEN SOMETHING IS OFF

When you don't have good health, you don't feel good. And when you don't feel good, you can become grumpy and moody. I've noticed that people often become more agitated as they get closer to the end of their lives. No matter their age, when someone passes from natural causes, there's often a shift—bitterness, crankiness, irritability. And not just in their final moments. Sometimes, it starts years earlier, even a decade before.

I don't just mean the elderly. I've seen this in younger people too. It's almost as if they're pushing people away. Maybe it's simply because they don't feel good. When the body is off, everything is off—mood, emotions, even outlook.

I've also noticed how a lack of sleep makes people unhappy. I know that sounds obvious, but my point is this: if something feels off within you, address it. Your health impacts your relationships, your thoughts, and your happiness.

If life feels off, check in with yourself. How do you feel? What hurts? Then take steps to fix it—because nothing else matters more.

You should feel good. You should move with ease. You should sleep well. You should feel happy. Sure, there will be tough days, but if you're constantly in pain, exhausted, or unhappy, something needs to change. Immediately.

SPECIAL MOMENTS

For me, it's important to turn those 4, 5, and 6 moments in life into something special. And even more important? Making those moments money-free or at least very inexpensive. Not just because of the whole five-kid thing but because I wanted to create memories, not buy them. That was part of the lesson I hoped to pass on.

I'd love to share some of my favorites with you. Feel free to try them out in your own life—see how they feel.

One of the first that comes to mind is enjoying a good rainstorm. For a while, it seemed to rain every day around 3:30. You could almost set your clock by it. I sometimes wonder what happened to those routine summer showers. We still get them, just not as regularly.

I love the way the sky darkens, the barometer drops, and the temperature dips. I love the way the wind picks up, the thunder booms so loud you can feel it in your chest. A good storm only lasts 15 to 30 minutes, so we had to act fast or we'd miss the best part—the very beginning, right as the rain starts to fall.

I would yell, "Storm!" and everyone would come running—out of their rooms, down the stairs. We'd turn off all the lights, light a candle, and head outside for as long as it was safe. When it got too wild, we'd watch the rest of the show from in front of the glass sliders (far enough back just in case—I hear you). We loved it.

Years later, after my kids moved out, they would still text me when a good storm was rolling through. I hope, even now, they still think of each other when it rains.

Another great memory was taking a picnic to Lake Mirror in Lakeland. It was about an hour's drive, so it felt like a special trip, not just an everyday outing. We usually went in the spring or fall when the weather was cool and crisp, with a nice breeze. We'd either pack a homemade lunch or grab Publix fried chicken or subs—plus some bread to feed the ducks and swans. (I know now that wasn't the best thing for them, but at the time, I had no idea.)

We'd spread out a couple of blankets under a shady tree and just be—soaking in the fresh air, the sounds of nature, and each other's company. This was before kids had cell phones, before any of us had the internet at our fingertips. Pretty sure this was around my pink Razr era. A favorite.

Once our bellies were full and the bread was gone, we'd head up to the playground for another hour. The kids would run, climb, and make new friends. This was no ordinary playground—it had a vibrant, sunflower-themed preschool area, complete with colorful turf, plus a labyrinth, a covered picnic space, and a multipurpose field.

Nearby, there was also a Splash Zone where water shot up from the ground, rained down from overhead, and even jumped from one side to the other. The kids loved trying to predict where the water would go next. We didn't go there often since we usually visited in cooler weather, but every once in a while, we'd add an extra hour or two for splashing fun.

This became one of their favorite childhood memories. Over the years, each of my kids has mentioned how much those outings meant to them. That makes my heart happy. I know they'll take their own children to places like this one day. In fact, one of my daughters, who's dating a guy with a son, has already made special memories of her own there. Eventually, they might find a different lake or park, but they'll create the same kind of magic for the next generation.

Another unforgettable experience was our trip to *Armature Works* when it first opened. An upscale food hall on the Tampa Riverwalk, it's housed in a historic building and features restaurants, an amphitheater, and a boardwalk. Outside, there are giant-sized games

PRACTICE *makes* POSITIVE

like chess and Connect Four, plus a park with sidewalks perfect for bikes, scooters, and carefree running. A lovely little stream runs through the center, and a local restaurant used to give out free fish food before installing a coin-operated dispenser. There's also a dog park and another Splash Zone.

We would spend the entire day there, and the kids felt like they were at a theme park. We had picnics, played games, explored, and just enjoyed the day. And the best part? We didn't spend a dime.

But one of my absolute best memories of all time? Our weekly Friday night dance parties.

We played the same favorite songs—our family theme songs—week after week. We'd crank up the volume (but not enough to annoy the neighbors), and we'd dance wildly in the living room. Silly moves, linked arms, dramatic spins, singing at the top of our lungs. It was the best!

And that's what I want you to take from all of this—just enjoy life. It doesn't take money. It doesn't take a lot of time. It just takes doing it.

Even something as simple as eating tacos on Cinco de Mayo can turn an ordinary day into a celebration. And also? Tacos will make you happy.

FINAL THOUGHTS ON HAPPINESS

Most people let their dreams pass them by, convinced that it takes too much time, effort, or money to reach them. And when life feels off, it becomes hard, unfulfilling—just work. It turns into everything you don't want. But I'm here to tell you that if you try hard enough, you can reach some level of your dream. Even a tiny corner of your aspirations will feel far better than a whole, sprawling life filled with things you don't love.

I believe that if you feel called to do something, you have some level of talent or affinity for it. I'm not saying you'll be the most successful person in the world at it, but you will be happy in that space. And happiness is a powerful thing.

When you're in alignment with what makes you feel alive, you'll want to try more things. Playfulness will surface. You'll wake up eager to start your day—even if it's just for that first sip of coffee in your favorite mug. The small nuisances of life won't bother you as much. You'll be kinder, and others will be kinder to you.

You'll recognize what serves you and what doesn't. You'll see and attract what makes you happy while naturally letting go of what doesn't. Life's gifts—the little moments that fall in your favor—will stand out more. And the more you embrace them, the more you'll notice.

You'll move through life lighter, happier, healthier, stronger. And when someone asks why you do things a certain way, you'll answer with confidence: "Because I like it that way." You'll smile, pull your shoulders back, and walk away with self-assurance. Even the work it takes to improve your life will feel like a joy because it's your life—one that reflects who you truly are.

You'll experience life instead of letting it pass you by. Your relationships will be more meaningful. Even challenges won't feel as defeating because you'll see alternative paths more clearly. You'll move more (because you'll be stretching and walking more), and you'll be at peace with who you are. You'll accept your limitations, celebrate your strengths, and seek out both teachers and students—finding inspiration and fulfillment in both.

With daily check-ins, staying in this flow will become easier. You'll recognize sooner when to walk away from something or embrace it fully. And if the entire world could live in this kind of harmony? Well, I imagine it would be utopia.

For me, it all boils down to gratitude. Gratitude for the challenges, the triumphs, and everything in between. You are here to experience it all. Every emotion you feel, every moment you live—it's all part of the gift.

So walk through your days with gratitude for everything that touches your world. Decide what you'll let in and what you'll simply observe. Learn. Love. Embrace life. Because if there's one universal truth, it's this: life moves fast. You should at least enjoy as much of it as you can.

And that's it. This is me. Thank you for spending this time with me. This is a glimpse inside my brain—not the most impressive place, I know, but it's my happy place. I hope something I've shared helps you create your own happiness. If not, pass this book along to someone who might need it and go on your way—no hard feelings.

I see you. I appreciate you. I wish you peace. But most of all,

I WISH YOU HAPPINESS.

Acknowledgments

Thank you to my best friends who believed in me enough that I believed in myself.

Thanks to Patti Yonteck and Kim Hardgrove for being the first ones to read my very first draft manuscript.

Thank you to Lauren Moore who read every version of the manuscript no matter how many do-overs.

Thank you to Michelle Sucher at Sucher Studio for designing the beautiful book cover.

Thank you to Jodi Costa at Shine Press Publishing for matching my energy and making this process fun.

Thank you to Susan Baracco for sticking with me to the very end and through all the hard parts. I would have never been able to do this without you!

Thank you to my children for being my reason, always.

Thank you to my husband, James, for being my constant supporter of 'what's next'.

Victoria Henrich
the author

Victoria Henrich was born and raised in sunny Florida and now calls Wesley Chapel home, where she lives with her husband and their three lively dogs. She is a fierce and loving mama of five children. She earned a bachelor's degree in Psychology from George Mason University and a Master of Science from Nova Southeastern University, always fueled by a passion for understanding people and what makes them thrive.

In 2011, Victoria took a leap and launched a branch of a staffing company—then took an even bigger leap by purchasing it in 2015. After years of dedication, she and her husband successfully sold the business in June 2024. During that transition, she wrote Practice Makes Positive as a way to channel optimism in the midst of uncertainty. Now, she's on a mission to spread that positivity, proving that with the right mindset, every challenge can lead to something greater.

CONNECT WITH VICTORIA

@practice makes
positive

@practice makes
positive

@livingyourvibration

@victoria henrich